The New
Cottage
Home

The New
Cottage
Home

JIM TOLPIN

The Taunton Press

To Cathy Parkman,

who gave up a most enchanting, wisteria-covered
town cottage to share my home and become my wife

Cover photo JIM MALECKI

Title-page photo JIM TOLPIN

Taunton
BOOKS & VIDEOS
for fellow enthusiasts

Text © 2000 by Jim Tolpin
Illustrations © 2000 by The Taunton Press, Inc.
All rights reserved.

Printed in the United States of America
10 9 8 7 6 5 4 3

The New Cottage Home was originally published in
hardcover in 1998 by The Taunton Press, Inc.

The Taunton Press, Inc., 63 South Main Street, PO Box 5506,
Newtown, CT 06470-5506
e-mail: tp@taunton.com

Distributed by Publishers Group West

Library of Congress Cataloging-in-Publication Data

Tolpin, Jim, 1947-.
    The new cottage home / Jim Tolpin.
        p.   cm.
    ISBN 1-56158-355-3 paperback
    1. Cottages—United States.   2. Architecture, Modern—20th
century—United States.   I. Title.
    NA7551.T65   1998
    728'.37'0973—dc21   97-48426
                                                            CIP

Read what critics have to say about *The New Cottage Home*

"Ah, a little home in the country. Jim Tolpin's *The New Cottage Home* will feed that fantasy, either intriguing you with what you could have or inspiring envy for what you don't."

—*Los Angeles Times*

"Whether you're looking for design inspiration for a new vacation home or you just want to look at stunning cottages and learn a little architectural history too, *The New Cottage Home* is a book to consider.... Features gorgeous photos, intriguing history, and practical construction details."

—*Today's Homeowner*

"In his book *The New Cottage Home*, Jim Tolpin builds a persuasive case for the warmth of a smaller house."

—*Coastal Living*

"A deliberate antidote to what the author calls 'a Madison Avenue drive toward continued conspicuous consumption.' ...[Tolpin] celebrates the compact and comfortable by looking at recent-vintage cottages in coastal and mountain areas, the forest, the open fields, and in town."

—*Associated Press*

"*The New Cottage Home* is designed to inspire flights of fancy about living a saner, simpler life in a snug little cottage in the woods, by the sea, or both."

—*Maine Times*

"...[a] fine and beautiful survey"

—*Pittsburgh Post-Gazette*

"Be forewarned...the designs, floor plans, and models selected by Tolpin are breathtaking and could spur a sudden burst of building and renovation."

—*Winnipeg Free Press*

"A delightful book for daydreaming about that little cottage in the woods you've always wanted.... Many of these 'cottages' look so lavish as to belie the humble origins of the name, but Tolpin provides a few dreams for every pocketbook."

—*Home & Garden Television online*

"Architects, interior designers, and students will find this book especially useful."

—*Library Journal*

"It takes only a drive through any typical American subdivision to confirm that in recent decades the average house has grown in size, narrowed in style, and shrunk in vision. Jim Tolpin's *The New Cottage Home* represents a return to a previous school of thought about living space... that it should pay homage to honest architecture and fine craftsmanship, not to conspicuous consumption. The 30 cottage homes pictured, all recently built, have the slightly unfair advantage of almost magically beautiful locations, but each has a unique character and many cottage-style nooks and crannies.... Tolpin does an excellent job of pulling together the elements of each that make it a cottage and make it appealing."

—*Amazon.com*

Acknowledgments

BRIAN VANDEN BRINK

I MUST FIRST ACKNOWLEDGE Seattle architect Geoffrey Prentiss, who, as we sat and talked in the saloon of his friend's beautiful sailboat, helped me steer this freshly conceived book in a more fruitful and personally satisfying direction. As the book developed, Stephanie Atwater helped me fine-tune some of the essential concepts, and Judith and Charles Landau introduced me to the work of Bernard Maybeck and other historical figures in cottage architecture. Once I had begun to write, reviewer Daniel Wing blessedly admonished me to remember to speak in my own voice, and architect Peter Wilcox, of Portland, Oregon, cleaned up many technical points.

Dean Coley, Ken Kellman, Dennis Britton, Clark Schultes, Michael Eckerman, Tom Rogers, John Ainley, Craig Savage, Carrie Grant, Sandor Nagyszalanczy, and Michele Bruns provided connections to many wonderful cottages and their creators. Nancy McCoy and Kiyo Oya of Morgantown and Coho communities on Lopez Island, Washington, took time from their busy lives to talk to me about their homes, make introductions, and walk me through their communities. In Carmel, Rain Wilmoth showed me some exemplary cottages and helped make photo arrangements. Speaking of photography, I am especially indebted to the two primary photographers in this book, Brian Vanden Brink and Craig Wester, and to the other photographers whose work helped bring this book to light and life. I would also like to thank Mike Kowalski for his charming watercolors and floor plans.

At The Taunton Press, I wish to acknowledge and thank Julie Trelstad, Karen Liljedahl, Jim Childs, Peter Chapman, Carol Singer, and Jodie Delohery, whose production efforts made this book possible.

Finally, I must also thank each of the architects and designers (listed at the back of the book) whose work graces these pages. Without them, *The New Cottage Home* would not exist.

Contents

Introduction 2

■ THE APPEAL
of the COTTAGE 4

■ A PORTFOLIO *of*
NEW AMERICAN COTTAGES 26

Cottages by the Water

A Fisherman's Camp Cottage 30

A Nantucket "Beach Box" 34

Far West Beach Cottage 40

A Down-East, Downsized, Shingle-Style Cottage 46

From Pumphouse to Beach Cottage 52

The Cottage on the Point 60

A Playhouse by the Sea 66

Cow Island Camp Cottage 76

Cottage Cluster East 82

BRIAN VANDEN BRINK

CRAIG WESTER

MICHAEL SKOTT

JOHN DANICIC, JR.

Cottages in the Field

A Little House for a Big Mountain *134*

A Modest Cottage on the Vineyard *140*

Island Cottage in Stone *144*

Stone Cottage Revival *150*

Salvage-Yard Vernacular *156*

A Cottage off the Grid *162*

Cottages of the Forest and Mountains

At Home on the Forest Trail *96*

A Tiny Temple in the Woods *102*

A Twin-Gabled Forest Cottage *106*

A French Hunting Lodge
in the Pacific Northwest *112*

A Cottage Made of Logs *116*

An Island Cottage on Spec *122*

A Cottage Cluster
in the Woods *126*

Cottages in Town

A Little Red House *172*

The Gray-Stone Cottage *176*

A Contemporary Cottage
in Connecticut *180*

The Town Cottages of
Stephen Wilmoth *186*

The Cottage as Community *196*

■ DESIGNING
the COTTAGE HOME *202*

Architects and Designers *230*

Introduction

(Practice) beautiful and appropriate architecture.

Do not build your dwelling-houses like temples, churches or cathedrals.

Let them be, characteristically, dwelling-houses...let the cottage be a cottage.

—Andrew Jackson Downing (writing in The Horticulturist, 1848)

FOR YEARS NOW, I've felt that many new homes reflect a Madison Avenue drive toward continued conspicuous consumption. From the 1960s into the mid-1990s, while the average American family shrank from 3.6 to 2.7 people, the size of the average new American house grew from 1,400 sq. ft. to 2,200 sq. ft. Even as families became smaller, many homes were built well beyond their practical needs. The increase in the size of our houses was matched only by the corresponding increase in our debt load (and in the subsequent rate of bankruptcies).

But as this century draws to a close, there seems to be a sea change in the way people are thinking about true wealth, true happiness, and the homes in which they want to live. At the same time our lives are becoming increasingly accelerated by the demands and trappings of the cybernetic future, many Americans find their hearts turning toward visions of a mellower and somehow more fundamental lifestyle. It seems we are finally ready to consider unpretentious, modest-sized houses that offer simplicity of form and construction;

that are less consumptive of resources and energy; and that so fit the landscape that they look like they were "grown" rather than built there. We are ready for houses that belong comfortably to their site and regional heritage—houses to which we, in turn, can comfortably belong.

In the pages that follow I present a tour of recently constructed houses whose design clearly evokes the feeling of "cottage" while still speaking to our contemporary lifestyle and to the architects' own visions. Each of these houses shares some, if not all, of the following attributes: a compactness of footprint, an informal and unpretentious interior, an exterior effusive in the use of indigenous materials and rich architectural details, and a site plan that responds intimately to the home's natural surroundings.

These houses seem to call as much to the heart as to the head, enriching us more with the highs of nature than with the highs of technology. These are the new American cottages that embody the ancient storybook dream, and the kind of homes that many of us have always dreamed of living in.

The Appeal of the
Cottage

Home and cottage—two words

most suggestive of comfort in the

English language...

—William H. Ranlett

(writing in *The Architect*, 1851)

Something about a diminutive window—especially one with shutters and a flowerbox—draws upon our most ancient, fondest memories of shelter. (PHOTO BY JIM TOLPIN.)

F OR MANY OF US, the archetypal image of the cottage home comes from storybook memories of our childhood: the diminutive dwelling glimpsed through the trees at the end of a winding trail, smoke rising from the chimney, roses rambling over a trellis and up onto the thatched roof above, leaded windows, an inviting entry…

There's something undeniably appealing about this image, something that makes the cottage the dream home for so many people today, but it's hard to put your finger on exactly what it is. After all, also implied in this picture are cramped quarters, perhaps a dark interior, and a lack of modern amenities. In attempting to define the enduring appeal of cottages, words like comfort, coziness, charm, simplicity, intimacy, and romance readily spring to mind, suggesting that the idea of "cottage" is as much a state of mind as it is a tangible presence.

To try to capture the essence of cottage appeal, think back to those most special places of your childhood. In your mind, revisit that snug hollow

(PHOTO FACING PAGE BY CRAIG WESTER.)

hidden under the dense lilac bush, the ramshackle fort cradled high in the limbs of the maple tree, the attic closet and its secret passageway winding under the stairs, or the bunk bed at the lake cabin draped with thick blankets. What do these places have in common? What did you feel like when you were in them? And what do these places of your childhood memories have to do with cottages?

I'll answer the last question for you—everything. For to me, these hollows, forts, and closets all evoke the essence of what the cottage house must be for us. In our childhood, we found or created spaces to fulfill an essential, unspoken need to feel safe and secure from an overstimulating and dangerous-feeling outside world. (If you think about it, none of these spaces would have felt this way had they been larger, more open to the outside, or more fancily built.) We may be all grown up now, but these needs are still essential to our sense of well-being. Those who understand this, understand the appeal of the cottage house:

One of the defining features of a cottage home is an exterior that rejoices in the use of indigenous materials and well-crafted, though perhaps quirky, architectural details. (PHOTO BY CARRIE GRANT.)

A magical, almost mysterious, place that holds us closely within its lovely boundaries, warming and soothing our work- and world-weary souls.

What seems to be a constant is the idea of the cottage as a calm retreat, the place to go to get away from it all—be it a beach cottage overlooking the ocean, a mountain hideaway, a pastoral retreat nestled in the woods or field, or even a thoughtfully built cottage in town. It's a place for lounging, for curling up with a good book, for napping, or for doing absolutely nothing. It's small enough to personalize and make your own: If you want to hang lobster pots from the ceiling or carve snail shells for drawer pulls, who's going to stop you?

The cottage as weekend/vacation getaway is only one aspect of the contemporary cottage. There's also the cottage as permanent residence—a perfect home for young marrieds, empty-nesters, retirees. (Many of the cottages featured in the portfolio section of this book are year-round, permanent residences.) The appeal here is a house that's easy to live in and easy to maintain, a house that encourages informal living while offering unpretentious comfort, a house that's small enough to allow you to spend more on fine details, quality materials, and craftsmanship, a house that's expressive about who you are and how you like to live your life.

The Cottage House

I hope I've helped you understand what a cottage feels like and why it's so appealing, but I'm sure you're still wondering what, exactly, makes one house just another house while another is—somehow—a "cottage." Admittedly, there's no hard-and-fast answer here: One person's cottage may be another person's hovel. But in selecting the houses that appear in this book, I looked for certain attributes—features that in some way evoke those spaces of childhood. Of course,

no one house offers all these attributes, but all the houses share many of these listed here:

- A modest-sized (under 2,000 sq. ft.), compact footprint that does not necessarily sacrifice a sense of spaciousness in the floor plan.
- A human-scale entry that welcomes you home.
- An unpretentious and intimate interior—most often centered around a hearth—in which you instantly feel warm, relaxed, and cozy.
- An exterior that makes good use of indigenous materials. Shingle siding, cedar-shake roofs, and fieldstone say "cottage"; vinyl siding paints quite a different picture.
- Well-crafted, sometimes quirky architectural details.
- The use of sashed windows—some diminutive in size— to reinforce the human scale of the building from the outside while giving a sense of security and protection to those on the inside.
- Thoughtful orientation of the building to the site and sun, relatively informal landscaping, and the presence of exterior "rooms" (porches, patios, decks)—all of which allow the house to respond to, and easily engage, its natural surroundings.

There are other attributes that come to mind—cozy nooks, high-pitched roofs, low ceilings, bare-wood floors, built-in furnishings, to name a few—but the seven characteristics listed above are, to me, the defining features of the small cottage home.

Going small is not done just for the sake of quaintness. Reducing volume also makes a structure energy- and resource-efficient, saving money—money that can go toward richer materials and the crafting of intimate, artful details inside and out. Architect Robert Gerloff of Minneapolis reminds his clients that it is the details that hold our interest, that can make the cottage "as unforgettable as a villa." And it is the details that give a home "a sense of charm, intimacy, and rightness"…and the ineffable sense of having been lovingly created by its builders.

A Brief History of Cottages

To appreciate why cottages are so popular and why architects and designer/builders continue to apply traditional cottage elements to contemporary houses, it helps to understand where the cottage forms and attributes come from. The cottage home has been with us for a very long time, but the idea of the cottage has changed dramatically over the centuries—from the humble hovel of the peasant farmer to the modest but enchanting family home or getaway of today. Along the way it has taken many forms, including the thatched-roof English cottage, the classic Cape Cod cottage, the Gothic Revival cottage, and the Arts and Crafts bungalow.

EARLY COTTAGES

We can trace the origins of the cottage back to the earliest primitive huts built around a hearth, but the first dwellings that most of us would recognize as cottages are the houses of medieval British and European serfs and servants (which were called "kots" in the old Norse language). While the ruling classes ensconced themselves in hugely magnificent, drafty castles built in the style of the hugely magnificent, drafty churches, the common folk lived modestly (and likely far more comfortably) in one- to two-room "mean-dwellings" intimately centered around a glowing hearth. Almost universally, these hovels were built of indigenous stone or timber and capped with a bowed or high-pitched thatched roof to shed away the rains.

Along with their rudimentary simplicity, many construction elements of these ancient hovels strike a chord with us today: The wattle and daub that filled the spaces between the wall posts we now express as textured plaster over wallboard. Eons of ducking through low doors set behind an arched roof overhang may account for our love of the intimate entryway. (The low door and arched roof were not there for style, of course. Instead, the squatness of the door kept the heat in, while the raised roofline prevented you from hitting your head on the thatchwork.) And those expansive, high-pitched roofs, thick with thatch, must take us back to the earliest times when shelter simply *was* a roof (and who could think to ask for more?). Indeed, we seem to sense that the more the roof, the cozier the home.

Then there is our seemingly illogical attraction to tiny windows—or at least to windows with multiple small panes. Perhaps this summons a remnant of memory that recalls the small windows of our first shelters: the "wind holes" that we occasionally left between the wattle and daub to let smoke out and fresh air in. Other fragments of memory inexorably draw us to exposed masonry foundations (perhaps to the rocks that held our earliest, flimsy bough structures to the earth) and, of course, to the rough-stone, fireside hearth—the center of our ancestral homes that has warmed us since the discovery of fire itself. It seems a good bet that our present-day cottage homes were more likely born from the ancient urgings of our first shelters and hovels than from the cold castles of the aristocracy.

THE QUINTESSENTIAL ENGLISH COTTAGE

By the mid-1600s in England, the common rural house—the form of shelter that has popularly become the quintessential "cottage"—had taken shape. No longer tiny hovels, these houses evolved to larger and more refined houses as a less-impoverished class of farmers and merchants arose to fill the void between the castled aristocracy and the unlanded peasantry. New knowledge and techniques of construction allowed the walls to move farther apart and roofs to soar higher. A house with a second story for sleeping had become commonplace. By the late 1800s, many of the cottages in rural England—in a romantic pursuit of the "picturesque"—had even become adorned with some of the embellishments of the aristocratic medieval past. It was not uncommon for a centuries-old cottage to be refurbished with leaded, diamond-pane windows, window hoods, and other Gothic-era elements.

Built throughout the English countryside since the late Middle Ages, stone-walled, thatched-roof dwellings have come to define the quintessential cottage home. (PHOTO BY BRIAN VANDEN BRINK.)

A scene out of the 1600s: Historically correct reproductions of the earliest dwellings of the Pilgrims march up the original hill site of Plimouth Plantation.

(PHOTO BY GARY ANDRASHKO; COURTESY PLIMOUTH PLANTATION.)

THE FIRST COTTAGES IN AMERICA

Not surprisingly, the early settlers in America built dwellings that harkened back to those they had left behind in England. We know from archaeological excavations at the site of the Plimoth Plantation in Plymouth, Massachusetts (and at other nearby sites) that the first colonists created small (440 sq. ft. or less) houses featuring massive oak corner posts set directly into the soil and a huge cobblestone hearth placed at one end. Written records of the plantation in Plymouth provide more details: By the first summer, the Pilgrims had constructed seven houses, all with white-oak timbers, thatched-reed or thatched-straw roofs, and riven-oak clapboard siding applied over wattle and daub. The wattle and daub was made by weaving saplings or rough-split boards around horizontal supports let into studs and then covered with a mixture of clay, sand, and straw. The addition of clapboards was essential since a lack of lime—an effective waterproofing additive—required that the daub be protected from the heavy New England rains.

THE CAPE COD COTTAGE

Within decades, settlers throughout the colonies busied themselves constructing homes—from the modest to the surprisingly lavish—in a variety of vernacularisms conveyed here from the motherlands. It wasn't until the late-18th century that a unique cottage form appeared in America. This was the now-ubiquitous single-gabled Cape Cod cottage created by settlers on Massachusetts's Cape Cod. Of course, those who built them were almost certainly not

The Peek House of Medfield, Massachusetts, built in 1680, is a good example of 17th-century English rural architecture in America. The tiny house features a high-pitched roof, which was probably thatched originally, and leaded-glass, diamond-pane, casement-type windows. (PHOTO BY ARTHUR C. HASKELL; COURTESY HISTORIC AMERICAN BUILDINGS SURVEY.)

The Rowell House of Wellfleet, Massachusetts, built in 1731, is one of the earliest surviving Capes and a prototypical half-Cape. Though similar in plan to the Peek House, it shows movement away from its medieval roots: The roof is not as steeply pitched, and the windows are sash-type, square lights rather than the archaic casement type with diamond-shaped leaded panes. (PHOTO COURTESY HISTORIC AMERICAN BUILDINGS SURVEY.)

thinking in terms of creating "cottage architecture" as we do. Instead, they aspired to build the largest homes they could afford to. For here in this new, vast land of freedom and opportunity the new Americans (many of whom had come from generations of unlanded peasants) saw a chance to create wealth: to own land and to build upon it dwellings similar to those of the affluent landed farmers and gentry of England. It would not be until the current century that words like "cute," "charming," or "cozy" would widely enter the language and imperatives of house design.

But many of the early houses of Cape Cod were small and, you must admit, charming. In the outlands of Cape Cod, materials and other resources were scarce and thus the houses were often more modest than elsewhere. A not uncommon variation of the standard-sized Cape was the "half-Cape," or "honeymoon cottage." Built on massive

THE HALF-CAPE

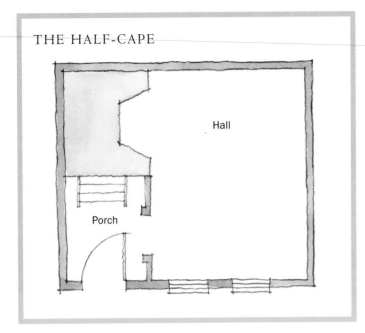

Hall

Porch

10x10 oak sills so the structure could be dragged on sand to other sites as the ubiquitous dunes shifted and changed the landscape, this diminutive house was early America's version of the starter home. Offering little more than an entry porch and a single room (the hall), the half-Cape was almost entirely devoid of adornment. This may not simply have been Puritan frugality, however: Projecting roof lines, window hoods, and other architectural appendages were easily damaged in the blustery ocean winds of the Cape.

What constitutes the classic Cape Cod house? Clair Baisly in her definitive *Cape Cod Architecture* (Parnassus Imprints, 1989) offers a number of identifying characteristics: In overall form, the archetypal Cape is a steep-roofed, asymmetrical fenestrated, story-and-a-half house with

THE CLASSIC CAPE

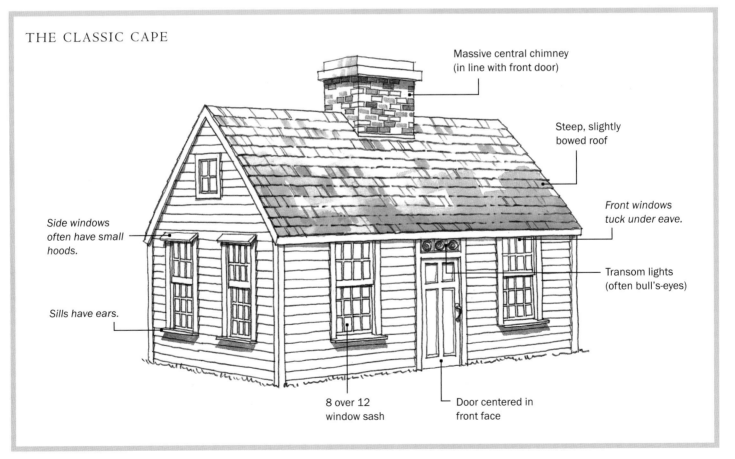

Massive central chimney
(in line with front door)

Steep, slightly
bowed roof

Front windows
tuck under eave.

Side windows
often have small
hoods.

Transom lights
(often bull's-eyes)

Sills have ears.

8 over 12
window sash

Door centered in
front face

single-gabled ends. Other features include small, multi-paned windows, a ridge-centered chimney placed directly in line with the front-entry door, and an absence of decorative exterior trim or ornamentation except for diminutive window hoods and transom lights (often bull's-eyes) above the entry door. Chimneys were monolithic with no decorative courses or segments. The walls were sided with either clapboard or shingle (never both). The land-scaping of the classic Cape would invariably include old-fashioned shrubs such as lilac, rose, and wisteria and often a mini-orchard of berry bushes and apple trees as well. This is also, perhaps, where the prototypical cottage's low, white picket fence originated.

Indeed, it is hard to deny the superb proportions of the classic Cape Cod house; the focus of its interior spaces on the massive hearth and chimney; its sense of repose as it sits rooted with natural stone to the earth; and the poignant framing of its form behind a profusion of antique flowers, shrubbery, and that picket fence. The classic Capes, whether by intent or not, represent one of America's most archetypal cottage-style houses, and they continue, in both style and essence, to influence our present urgings to create a contemporary, yet quintessential, cottage home.

GOTHIC REVIVAL COTTAGES

The cottage form, transferred to these shores through both necessity and architectural innocence, soon became a style in itself. By the 1840s the Romantic movement was exerting itself across the country, fueled in part by the Hudson River school of art and the widely read poetry of Keats, Wordsworth, Goethe, and Poe. Those eager to invoke the romanticism thought to be embodied in the cottage-like home came to rely for inspiration on innovative, relatively low-cost house-plan books that capitalized on the trend. Here one could find enticing line drawings and generalized floor plans of vernacular European small-home styles, primarily English rural cottages and Swiss chalets.

A typical plan-book house, this one from from *Village and Farm Cottages* by H. W. Cleaveland and William and Samuel Bachus (1856), offered the common man and his family an affordable yet charming home.

The first of these books published in the United States—*Rural Residences*—was put forth by architect Alexander Jackson Davis in 1837. Later, his student and subsequent collaborator Andrew Jackson Downing would publish the widely read *Victorian Cottage Residences* (1842) and *The Architecture of Country Houses* (1850), both of which are still in print today. Other architects such as Henry Cleaveland and William and Samuel Bachus produced plans for even more modest homes aimed at workers and "mechanics." But even these humble dwellings achieved an air of "romantic picturesque" as many builders embraced the architects' suggestions to install eave brackets, verandas with corbels, fancy chimney caps, window hoods, and board-and-batten siding.

This architectural period, achieving its golden years just before the Civil War, has come to be known as the era of Gothic Revival. It arguably presents us with our deepest reservoir of ideas in domestic, cottage-style architecture.

A typical design offering of Downing's, this small cottage utilizes many elements to achieve its picturesque quality: irregular form, bracketed roof overhang, bold window trim, gables over the door and window, a bay window, exterior seating, trellises, and a segmented chimney.

The Delameter House of Rhinebeck, New York, built in 1844, adhered closely to a plan-book design from Alexander Jackson Davis's *Rural Residences*.

(PHOTO BY BRIAN VANDEN BRINK.)

Andrew Jackson Downing's ideas were hugely influential in their day and are still highly relevant to the contemporary American cottage. While Downing was the leading proponent of Gothic Revival cottages, he had already made his reputation—and probably most of his income—from the design of villas, manors, and country houses for the well-to-do. But in the decades before the Civil War, he had come to see it as his task "to find a suitable domestic architectural style for his fellow Americans."

While venerating the honest vernacularism of the classic English cottage, Downing acknowledged that the re-creation of these typically large English houses was generally inappropriate for the working classes of America. Instead, he believed that the architecture of the American everyman should go beyond a particular archetype to embrace the basic principle of simplicity—an imperative that "ought, accordingly, to pervade every portion of cottage architecture." He proposed that there must be a "simplicity of arrangement to facilitate the simple manner of living, simplicity of construction, tasteful simplicity of decoration to harmonize with the character of the dwelling and its occupants"—an imperative that has been embraced by many contemporary architects. At the same time, his designs abounded in delightful details and are anything but simple to modern aesthetics.

Downing's bottom line was to attempt to combine studied taste with the modesty, simplicity, and truth of "cottage life." In doing so, he hoped to give the common American a delightful, meaningful (and, yes, even romantic) place in which to live.

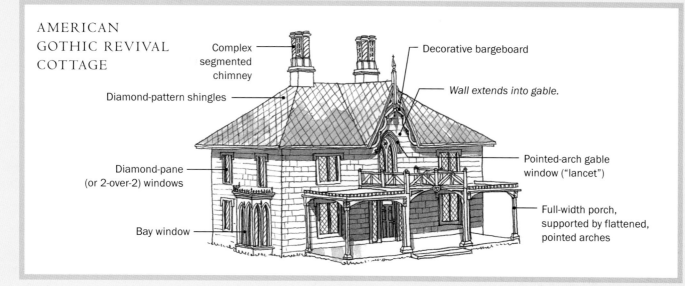

AMERICAN
GOTHIC REVIVAL
COTTAGE

Complex segmented chimney

Diamond-pattern shingles

Diamond-pane (or 2-over-2) windows

Bay window

Decorative bargeboard

Wall extends into gable.

Pointed-arch gable window ("lancet")

Full-width porch, supported by flattened, pointed arches

Andrew Jackson Downing's Design Principles for the Gothic Revival House

In his house designs, Downing strove to enact two basic principles: utility (in which he acknowledged that a house should first and foremost be comfortable—a relatively new concept in thinking about homes) and beauty (in which he implied that beauty derives only from "truth" in function and form). For Downing, and for fellow small-home designers, the design challenge was to strike just the right balance so that "the useful should never be sacrificed to the ornamental... (and that) beauty should grow out of the former."

PRINCIPLES OF UTILITY

1 The principal entrance or front door should never open directly into a room but always into a porch or entry of some kind.
2 The roof should always be steep enough to shed snow freely.
3 The level of the first floor should be at least 1 ft. off the ground to ensure dryness.
4 The kitchen—and thus the joys of home life—should always be on the first floor (not in the basement as it is placed in classical homes).

5 There should be some form of insulation to make the house snug against the winter cold.

PRINCIPLES OF BEAUTY

1 Strive for simplicity of outline and regularity in proportion and symmetry—though some asymmetry is acceptable to make the cottage more picturesque.
2 Add ornament tastefully (so as not to destroy the simplicity of the basic premise of the structure) to the most important parts of the building, such as the entrance door, principal windows, gables, and chimneys.

3 Add domestic touches (such as porches, verandas, simple bay windows, outdoor benches) rather than tacked-on ornaments, which detract from the honesty of cottage life.
4 Paint the house. White is a good choice because it is highly reflective to sunlight and thus better protects the underlying wood.
5 Landscape the cottage surrounds. Proper landscaping can do far more to create and sustain the cottage home than can any kind or amount of contrived ornamentation.

A mansard roof-style cottage, tiny by Victorian-era standards, sits modestly amidst its garden. (PHOTO BY JIM TOLPIN.)

POST-CIVIL WAR COTTAGES

In the years following the Civil War, the influence of romanticism upon the American mind declined—fatally punctured, perhaps, by the gross realities of war and the struggles of Reconstruction. The majority of postwar homebuilding shifted away from medieval Gothic influences—even though the soon-to-be-pervasive Victorian architecture began with the application of French or Italian classic detailing to medieval forms. But only the smallest versions of these and other Victorian-style dwellings seem to capture the flavor and intent of the home as envisioned by the romanticism of Gothic Revival. It is ironic—or perhaps perverted wishful thinking—that the largest and most

Carpenters of East Coast religious "meeting camps" delighted in creating tiny, whimsical cottages in as high-Gothic a style as they could afford. (PHOTO BY BRIAN VANDEN BRINK.)

ostentatious of these Victorian mansions were called "cottages" by their affluent inhabitants.

By the end of the 19th century, the Victorians' imperious emphasis on the grand had led most architects away from the creation of smaller, more prosaic dwellings. However, pockets of cozy, visually delightful, true cottage-like homes could still be found under construction in certain regions of the country. The tiny, almost festive, cottages of East Coast religious meeting camps were a delightful revival of the earlier Gothic era. Their stylized facades not only invoked the sacred imagery of medieval cathedrals but also added a spirit of playfulness and community to the summer gatherings. In these camp cottages, we can see the beginnings of the idea of the cottage both as retreat and as clustered community.

In the South, local house builders applied Victorian-style spindlework to the vernacular "folk" homes still being built into the last half of the 19th century. This design strategy proved particularly enchanting on the long, single-room-width "shotguns" of New Orleans. The lavish addition of prefabricated ornamentation imbued these modest and otherwise plain-looking houses with life. For their owners, working people of modest means, these dwellings became homes with delightful personalities, homes with a sense of place that one could enjoy and respect, homes that fit the definition of "cottages."

A typical "shotgun"-style house, delicately ornamented only on its street face, fills a long, narrow lot in turn-of-the-century New Orleans.

(PHOTO COURTESY OF THE HISTORIC NEW ORLEANS COLLECTION.)

A gallery of cottages built
between 1900 and 1938 in the
Monterey Bay area of California.

(PHOTOS BY JIM TOLPIN.)

CRAIG WESTER

On the West Coast, from the turn of the century until the 1930s, a wave of Gothic Revival cottages proliferated throughout the Monterey Bay area of California. These small settlements, at that time mostly blue-collar beach towns, could offer the majority of their inhabitants only the tiniest of building lots. The sites quickly became festooned with tents, rough log-faced cabins, or innovative, tiny, hexagonal houses. But soon, more money and imagination flowed into the area. In Carmel especially, those seeking to create a classic Gothic-style cottage seaside retreat engaged the vision and hands of builders such as Hugh

Comstock. Drawing upon the renderings of British illustrator Arthur Rackham—and probably the plan books of Alexander Downing and other popular architects of the first Gothic Revival—Comstock created a number of cottages that kept the short-lived resurgence well fed.

THE BEGINNINGS OF MODERNISM

Elsewhere in America at the turn of the century, however, a movement was well afoot in the architectural community that reacted forcefully and innovatively against the last century's ubiquitous preoccupation with historical revivalisms. Architects like Frank Lloyd Wright sought new ways of building that would be more appropriate for an industrial society emerging into a new, "modern" century. As such, they did away with the traditionalist's strong symmetrical forms, complex textures and colors, and applied ornamentation until their work represented the antithesis of nearly all of American architecture since the passing of vernacularism at the end of the 1700s.

At first glance, this new architectural style would seem to have little to do with cottage homes. But although much of the residential work was large in scale, the design concepts of Frank Lloyd Wright in particular would prove to be of great importance in the design of the comfortable, spacious-feeling small house. For it was Wright who pushed the American house away from segmented rooms that physically and visually cut themselves off from one another and from the surrounding exterior landscape. Strongly influenced by Japanese houses (which are characterized almost entirely by contiguous spaces), Wright's long, low "Prairie" style houses (and, later, the smaller "Usonian" houses) exalted in their sense of openness and in their enthusiastic embracing of the space immediately surrounding the house.

One of Frank Lloyd Wright's typical "Usonian" houses, the Pope-Leighey House, a property of the National Trust for Historic Preservation, is a diminutive 1,200 sq. ft. The small scale and budget of this house forced Wright to pare the project to the bone while making the space both functional and thoroughly enjoyable to live in. (PHOTO COURTESY THE NATIONAL TRUST FOR HISTORIC PRESERVATION, WOODLAWN PLANTATION.)

It was Wright and his contemporaries who gave us kitchens opened to dining rooms, living rooms embracing cozy dens, two-story spaces united by light wells, and decks serving as continuums of interior living areas—current architectural paradigms that are easily taken for granted. For it is precisely these design elements, as we shall see in abundance in the portfolio section of this book, that imbue the compact spaces of today's cottage homes with a far different feel than that of their European and mid-1800s American Gothic Revival ancestors.

THE ARTS AND CRAFTS BUNGALOW

Concurrent with the infusion of modernism into American high architecture was the widespread adaptation of yet another English design trend: the Arts and Crafts movement, a "low architecture" for the everyman. Stressing affordability and modesty in form and ornament, this movement oversaw the resurgence of the design and creation of small, but extraordinarily appealing and functional homes for the average American worker.

Called "bungalows"—a term apparently derived from the similar-shaped "bangla" thatched-roof cottages of British-occupied India—these one or one-and-a-half story homes were typically square-shaped and compact. Broad, graceful roofs embraced the bungalow, their generous overhangs sheltering the side walls and the ubiquitous porches. Sloping stone foundations, massive porch columns, and exposed timber-framing gave the houses a firm sense of stability and security, while decorative stickwork, braces, transom windows, and extensive built-in furnishings lent much charm and functionality to these modest homes.

Like the earlier Gothic Revival cottages and the Southern shotguns, Arts and Crafts bungalows were rich with a sense of personality and place. They were homes that families of modest means could feel drawn to, proud of, and truly a part of.

THE COTTAGE ARCHITECTURE OF BERNARD MAYBECK

Before we begin our tour of contemporary cottages, there's one last designer/craftsman who deserves special mention for his contribution to the cottage form. In the hillsides of Berkeley, California, in the early decades of this century, bohemian architect Bernard Maybeck drew on both the Arts and Crafts movement and the earlier Gothic Revival archetypes to create homes that would offer a fitting response to the ostentatious mansions of San Francisco. Maybeck stated unequivocally that he hated "white-painted houses with nailed-on ornament"—a description that fit nearly all Victorian homes in America. Later, when the

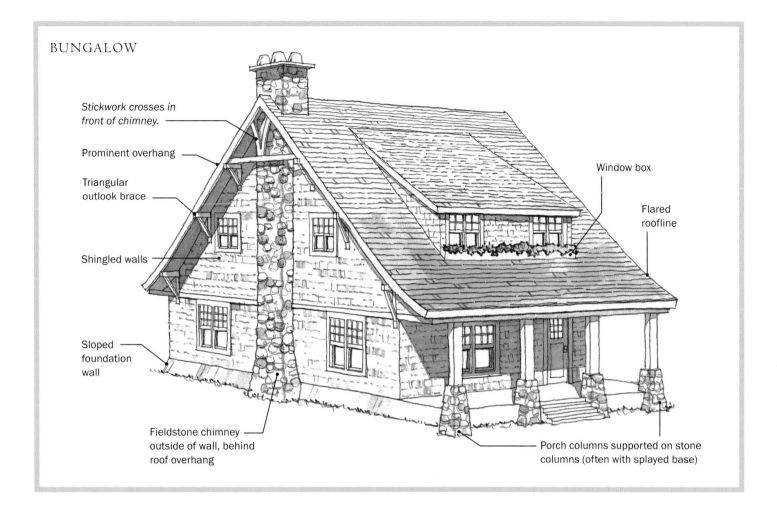

BUNGALOW

Stickwork crosses in front of chimney.

Prominent overhang

Triangular outlook brace

Shingled walls

Sloped foundation wall

Fieldstone chimney outside of wall, behind roof overhang

Window box

Flared roofline

Porch columns supported on stone columns (often with splayed base)

Victorian era finally succumbed, Maybeck said it died of a "dreadful absence of beauty."

Maybeck's architecture was dominated by his search for "truth"—a search that drew him to a profound exploration and reverence of medieval Gothic architecture. He came to believe that "medieval architecture exemplified architectural truth because it was made by craftsman who used materials according to their inherent qualities." This understanding led Maybeck (and many of his contemporaries) to give renewed importance to the structural elements of the building, to emphasize them (rather than applied elements) as the "ornaments" of the design. Indeed, Maybeck ascribed

to the notion that the sacred architecture of the Gothics embraced a vast body of universal truths that were made manifest in the harmonious proportions and structural arrangements of their buildings. He felt, for example, that certain repetitions of exposed columns and rafters might also correlate to the consonant beats of music or the metrical accents of classic poetry.

The small, quality homes that came from the heart, mind, and, in some cases, the hands of Bernard Maybeck benefited enormously from his relentless quest for architectural truths. As long-time admirer Richard Sexton summarized in *The Cottage Book* (Chronicle Books, 1989): "His

The yearning for the cottage isn't necessarily a solitary quest for a quiet, rustic retreat. Instead, the cottage home—when drawn into clusters—can hold the promise of a rich life filled with the joys of residing in a meaningful, safe community.

It is no secret that many of us are drawn to this lifestyle. As tourists, we swarm by the millions through towns such as Nantucket, Massachusetts, Portsmouth, New Hampshire, and Charleston, South Carolina, marveling at the quaint houses that closely line the narrow streets.

What are the promises being whispered to us here? What is it that so

The Cottage as Community

In community we seek strength and a sense of belonging...

—Clair Baisly, *Cape Cod Architecture*

inexorably draws us to these classic American communities? Perhaps it is those narrow streets, which, we suddenly realize, were designed for people, not automobiles. Or perhaps it is the closeness of the houses to the sidewalks (with only a picket fence to define a gentle boundary) that makes the entire street feel like a friendly, shared room.

It is this same feeling of neighborliness and belonging that is fueling the development of cottage communities all over the country. In marked contrast to the isolated dwellings of the suburbs, houses in cottage communities cluster close together, often around a commonly owned "village green." Cars are parked well away from this central space. Porches draw people outside and encourage interactions with passing neighbors.

In these people-oriented communities, the residents are respected by the houses and the streets themselves and are thus encouraged to greet, help, and respect one another. It is here, in the midst of a cottage community, that many people are sensing that they might, for once, feel completely at home.

(PHOTO ABOVE BY CRAIG WESTER.)

houses possess the human qualities we closely associate with cottages...a sense of rightness anchored in traditional, heartfelt values."

According to Maybeck's daughter-in-law Jacomena, his homes were strongly vernacular to "evoke a strong sense of the past...to keep one in tune with the environment—the garden, the breeze, the sun, the elements of nature." His homes were focused on the outside to gardens (he often incorporated planters and trellises into house design) and on the inside to the hearth. Vaulted ceilings supported with Gothic structures evoke a reverence for their medieval roots while imbuing the rooms with spaciousness and light (see, for example, the photo on p. 226). There's a strong emphasis on wood looking like wood—unusual in an era where anyone of means lived in homes filled with decorative overlays and coverings.

THE NEW AMERICAN COTTAGE

In the years following World War II, the cottage home seemed headed for decline, eclipsed by the flood of modern- and International-style houses that were sweeping across the American landscape. In nearly every corner of the country, the derivative ranch-style home seemed to fill every vacant field and town lot. Ranch houses offered the burgeoning middle class an affordable, clean, dry (but all-too-often boring) box in which to live. These were houses that were a far cry from the dank caves of our Paleolithic ancestors but a sad cry from the heart- and eye-satisfying homes of the American romanticists and craftsman-artists of the 19th and early 20th centuries.

It has been only in the last few decades that there has been any significant return to the well-crafted, modest-sized house—a return to well-designed and well-built homes that fill and enrich us with their unique sense of personality and place. It is to these cottage homes that have recently come to be built by the water, in the forests, fields, and towns of America that I devote the balance of this book. I hope you'll enjoy the tour.

This house, built in 1916 in Forest Hill, California, is rich in English Gothic detailing yet acknowledges its presence in the New World with unusual, light-filled rooms, such as the polygonal-shaped sleeping porch on the second floor. (PHOTO BY RICHARD BARNES.)

A Portfolio of New American Cottages

To harmonize with the surrounding scenery,

to enter into the spirit of the landscape,

is the highest beauty of a domestic building.

—J. J. Thomas

(writing in *The Register of Rural Affairs*, 1865)

Cottages
by the Water

There's something deeply comforting about a cottage by the water. It's the place where you can really get away from it all, where you can unwind with a good book, canoe across a lake shimmering with the sunset, or just hunker down on the porch to listen to the murmur of the evening zephyrs. Whether by the surging sea, a tranquil lake, or a babbling brook, the waterside cottage is truly the quintessential retreat.

A Fisherman's Camp Cottage

It wasn't easy for the Uptons to build their dream cottage—a year-long product of working part time between commercial fishing seasons and rearing two small children. Construction materials came slowly as spare cash was squeezed out of the family budget. Runs to salvage yards and flea markets became a weekend ritual, though some materials, such as the large beam that supports the second story, were found nearby the camp site.

Not only was the cottage built on a shoestring, it was designed with one too. Instead of a formal set of plans, the Uptons sketched the outline and rough floor plan of the camp literally on the back of an envelope while sitting at the kitchen table. After the deck was built, Joe set up sticks and ran strings to indicate the potential locations of doors and windows. Walking around the deck, he and his wife Mary Lou would look through the strings, carefully contemplating the view through the "windows" and the path through the "doors." When they were satisfied, up went the framing to forever commit the walls to these openings.

SIZE 1,000 sq. ft.; COMPLETED 1982; LOCATION Vinalhaven, Maine; DESIGNER/BUILDER Joe and Mary Lou Upton; PHOTOGRAPHER Brian Vanden Brink

camp cottage, sitting on a small swell of land surrounded by marsh and sea, provides a cozy and economical summertime retreat for a family of four.

The simple shapes of the structure and dormer not only saved the Uptons time and money but also allowed the cottage to blend with the ubiquitous Cape Cod–style homes of the island. The generous overhangs—a deviation from those of typical Capes—protect the windows and side walls from constant exposure to fog drip. The expansive deck quickly became the children's play yard.

covered in wood, the house has the feel of a rustic camp cottage. To lighten the walls (and the overall tone of the room), the Uptons "pickled" the white-pine wall boards by brushing on a highly thinned washcoat of white paint and then immediately wiping it off with rags.

Many of the salvaged materials from which the house was built are in evidence here: the large summer beam wrenched out of a collapsed barn on the other side of the island, the hearth of recycled bricks, and the southern hard pine floor.

like the floor, are constructed from richly textured southern pine, giving the light-filled space a homey glow. A massive enamel drainboard-style sink, also salvaged from the junkyard, fills one counter. The breakfast-bar counter has a wide knee-space rather than an overhang so as not to encroach on the living room.

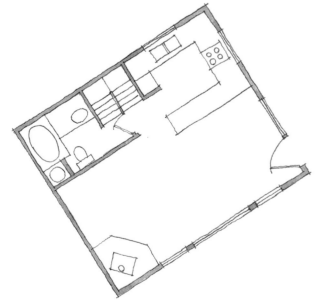

THE PERKY SHED-ROOF dormer provides ample room for the children's bedroom. To cut costs and to bring more light into the diminutive space, the Uptons chose to cover the walls with drywall rather than with wood. Beach-combed lobster-pot buoys fill the room, not to mention the children's dreams and summertime memories, with a splash of color.

a fisherman's camp cottage **33**

A Nantucket "Beach Box"

OUTWARDLY, THERE'S NOTHING that remarkable about this diminutive beach cottage on Nantucket Island, off the coast of Massachusetts. Its simple, shingled form closely follows the traditional boxed shape of the earliest shelters on the island. What is remarkable is that a structure this modest got built at all given the prime status and cost of this lovely piece of oceanfront real estate.

The average Nantucket client comes to the island with plenty of money and a long list of requirements for gracious living. But the owners of this beach cottage approached architects Raymond Pohl and Lisa Botticelli with a rather atypical program: "Build for our family of four a modest, uninsulated, unheated cottage with a spartan floor plan that includes only one open room for living and cooking, a bedroom for the adults, and a single bathroom. The children will happily sleep in cots flanking the fireplace." Following the clients' lead, the architects gave them a house strongly linked to the island's landscape and heritage.

SIZE 1,100 sq. ft.; COMPLETED 1995; LOCATION Nantucket, Massachusetts; DESIGNER Raymond Pohl and Lisa Botticelli; BUILDER Bruce Killen; PHOTOGRAPHER Claudia Kronenberg

LIKE THE BEACH SHANTIES cobbled together by 18th-century whalers, the cottage sits on piers rather than on a continuous wall foundation. This allows the occasional ocean surge to run under the house with little resistance, rather than carry the structure away. It also allows the house to be moved around on the property to accommodate shifting, eroding dunes.

Typical Nantucket beach-cottage features include shingles that meet at the corners of the house instead of butting into a corner board, a massive chimney that tapers toward the bottom, and lightning rods with blown-glass insulators.

rafter tails introduce a subtle, but welcome, relief from the building's Puritan-plain forms. The exterior red-cedar trim is left untreated, to weather to a soft silver-gray in the sun and salt air.

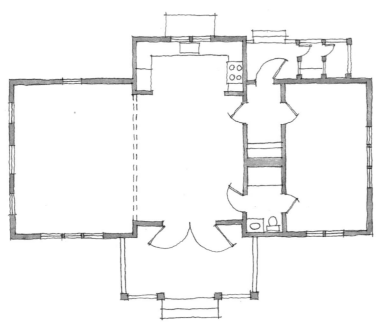

a modest cottage

on one of the world's prime stretches

of oceanfront real estate...

tucks into an alcove on the back of the house with virtually no separation from the great room. The exposed beaded panel on the back of the upper cabinets—an archetypal cottage element—covers wiring and plumbing, as do shiplapped pine boards. The white-painted wood cabinets, with full-recess doors and drawer faces, were built on site.

THE VAULTED CEILING AND uncovered walls expose custom-milled roughsawn spruce framing. The designers specified that the lumber be removed from the mill before the customary final step of planing to maintain a more textured finish. The result was framing stock thicker than standard dimensions, featuring prominent mill marks and crisp edges. The floors were finished with salvaged antique "pumpkin pine" boards.

Cables and thin metal turnbuckles replace more traditional collar ties—a strategy to make the interior of this small house feel more open and spacious.

THE DINING AREA IS BATHED in natural light from the cluster of windows set under the cross gable. In good weather, you can swing the barn-type doors outward—the screen doors sit on the inside— to enjoy a sweeping view of the sea.

The tastefully simple chandelier looks like a bouquet of candles, in keeping with the primitive nature of this cottage and setting.

Far West Beach Cottage

THIS MODEST CALIFORNIA BEACH COTTAGE, built in the 1930s, has been in the same family for most of its life. Over the years, the owners had grown comfortable with its unpretentious, familiar nature, but there were more than a few quirks that cried out for attention. The kitchen had an awkward step down from the living room, and its low ceiling made it feel dark and cramped. The placement of the bathroom was also a point of frustration and missed opportunity: If it was moved, the cottage could finally be opened to a view of the surf running north along the beach.

Familiar with some of architect Andy Neumann's many beach cottages in the area, the owners called him in to oversee an extensive makeover. Neumann sensed a challenge: He must make the place feel more comfortable and convenient without destroying the easy informality of the family's beach haven.

SIZE 2,176 sq. ft.; COMPLETED 1995; LOCATION Carpenteria, California; DESIGNER Andy Neumann, Carpenteria, California; BUILDER Frank Louda (Chismahoo Construction); PHOTOGRAPHER Andy Neumann

A PATH OF FLAGSTONES
winding through a pro-
fusion of flowers leads
you into this 1930s-era
California cottage-retreat
on the sea.

Though much of the
house has enjoyed an ex-
tensive remodel, it still has
the look and feel of the
original. Elements that
have been retained include

the quirky rain hood over
the French doors and the
covered walkway to the
side of the house.

The refurbished,
straightforward trimwork
is in keeping with the relaxed modesty of a beach
cottage. The structure to
the right is the garage,
trimmed and painted to
match the house.

is essentially one large room with bedrooms placed in wing extensions. The furniture in the foreground clusters around the windows that overlook the ocean. A second set of chairs (in the background) provides cozy, after-dark seating by the fire.

The kitchen, to the left behind the raised counter, opens upward to its newly trussed cathedral ceiling, gaining far more sense of space than the original kitchen could muster with its dark, low ceiling. The trusses in the great room are original, as is the pine paneling.

Bottom: A generous view from the kitchen takes in the dining area as well as the hearth.

The uniform color of the walls and trim...enhances the room's sense of simplicity and serenity.

AFFECTIONATELY CALLED "the slot," the corridor running from the living room to the master-bedroom wing is the perfect place to bed down surprise drop-ins and overnight guests. Two beds placed end to end share a full-length guardrail and pull-out storage beneath.

The original board-and-batten interior wall surface (here and in the master bedroom) was replaced with plywood and battens to increase the structural strength of the walls. To avoid the look of plywood, Neumann specified a grade of plug-free plain-sawn plywood. It is nearly impossible to determine that the walls are not wide boards with batten-covered seams.

THE MASTER-BEDROOM WING is farthest from the water (which allows the communal space to take full advantage of the sea-facing side of the house). The uniform color of the walls and trim—off-white to maximize the diffusion of northern light—enhances the room's sense of simplicity and serenity. The painted linen cupboard, purposely small in scale, adds tasteful contrast of color.

To preserve and reinforce the ambiance of a beach-cottage retreat, Neumann had the carpenters only partially strip the paint from the original ceiling boards. The result is a ceiling that recalls its origins as beachcombed lumber.

of the 19th century, Neumann gave the craftsmen involved free rein to resolve some of the architectural detailing.

The inspired Dutch-style entry, constructed with a mortise-and-tenon frame set around beaded solid-wood planks, boasts a porthole-style window and a gracefully arched top. A satisfying resolution of the curved-top casing trim joins the door frame's side stiles. Boards carefully sawn to a curve and through-bolted with bronze fasteners tastefully capture and trim out the round piece of glass.

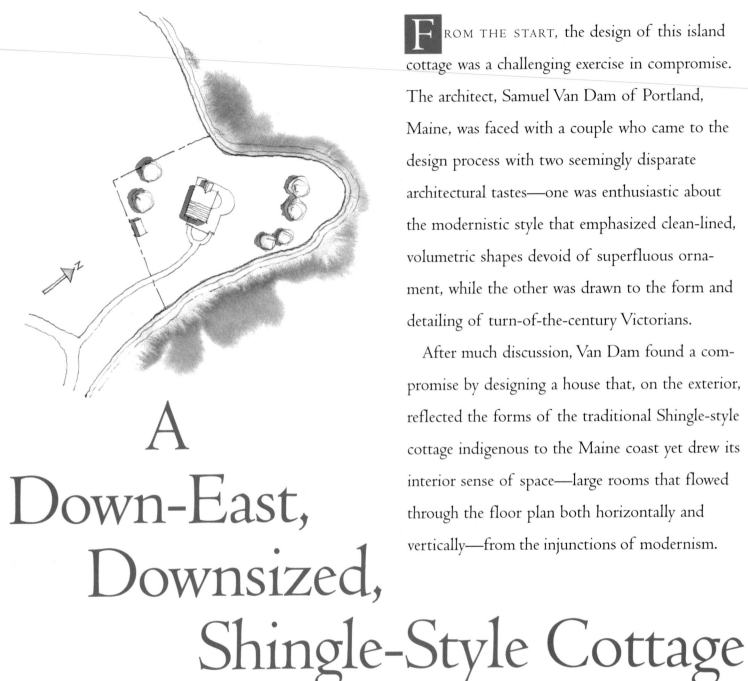

A Down-East, Downsized, Shingle-Style Cottage

$\mathbf{F}$ROM THE START, the design of this island cottage was a challenging exercise in compromise. The architect, Samuel Van Dam of Portland, Maine, was faced with a couple who came to the design process with two seemingly disparate architectural tastes—one was enthusiastic about the modernistic style that emphasized clean-lined, volumetric shapes devoid of superfluous ornament, while the other was drawn to the form and detailing of turn-of-the-century Victorians.

After much discussion, Van Dam found a compromise by designing a house that, on the exterior, reflected the forms of the traditional Shingle-style cottage indigenous to the Maine coast yet drew its interior sense of space—large rooms that flowed through the floor plan both horizontally and vertically—from the injunctions of modernism.

SIZE 1,470 sq. ft.; COMPLETED 1987; LOCATION Cushing Island, Maine; DESIGNER Samuel Van Dam, Portland, Maine; BUILDER Fine Lines Construction, Yarmouth, Maine; PHOTOGRAPHER Bob Perron (except where noted)

you notice as you approach the cottage is the row of white-painted columns that march across the front porch. These supports, though unadorned, evoke a touch of grandeur from the golden age of the Shingle-style cottage. At the same time, they echo the white-barked birches surrounding the house.

The porch wraps around both sea-facing sides of the house and repeats the shape of the dining room, effectively extending the living room into the out-doors. The second-floor porch offers privacy and an unhindered view across the water.

JAMIE SALOMON

THE SHARP ROOF LINES
and the rather subtle
gambrel applied to the
back half of the roof
offer further reminders
of the Shingle era.

To make the most of
the sun, Van Dam extended
the tall windows well up
into the gable, allowing
light to flow from floor to
floor and into the core of
the house.

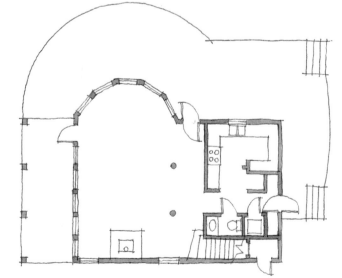

THE FIRST FLOOR'S HIGH ceiling contributes to the cottage's sense of spaciousness. The exposed wall and ceiling framing soften the formality of the Shingle style, helping the interior feel casual and cozy. The pickled white finish infuses the space with a soft luminescence, which prompted one visitor to say that entering the room was "like walking into an Andrew Wyeth watercolor."

The columns carry the theme of the porch supports inside and also help define the edge of the living room area by creating a sense of separation from the traffic path leading to the side-entry door.

"...like walking into an Andrew Wyeth watercolor"

THE KITCHEN DEFINES ITS territory with a half-wall to create a niche off the great room—style living room. Its white-painted cabinets are unobtrusive and pleasingly informal. The box standing away from the wall by the entry door encloses a fridge and creates space behind for a hall closet.

The large transom window over the kitchen entry door (just visible at the right edge of the photo) brings southeast light deep into the core of the house and jogs up into the second floor to become a window seat.

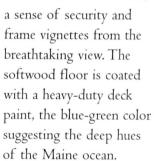

THE WALL-TO-WALL ROW of 2-over-2 windows draws the view into the room, while substantial solid-wood mullions lend a sense of security and frame vignettes from the breathtaking view. The softwood floor is coated with a heavy-duty deck paint, the blue-green color suggesting the deep hues of the Maine ocean.

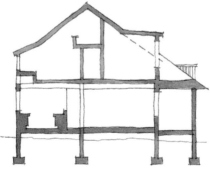

BY HOLDING THE SECOND floor away from the southwest-facing wall, Van Dam made it possible for the windows to extend unbroken up the gable end. This strategy not only illuminates the stairway but also fills the entire house with daylight and a feeling of great expanse.

From Pumphouse to Beach Cottage

I T WAS AN APPEALING SITE for a beach cottage. Unfortunately, a very unappealing building was already sitting on it: an odd-shaped, flat-roofed, 433-sq.-ft. pumphouse building.

The client's intent was to create a permanent, simple (but lavishly crafted) dwelling for one out of the old pumphouse. Architect Geoffrey Prentiss was delighted to take on the challenge, especially in this situation where "money ordinarily consumed to create 'space' could instead be used to accomplish 'quality' in construction, details, and finish."

Because increasing the size of the building was out of the question, Prentiss worked instead on increasing the perception of space: He angled the flat ceiling upward to the 90° corner, placed a bank of casement windows toward the water, designed the cabinetry for maximum storage and minimal intrusion, and created a huge deck around two-thirds of the house.

SIZE 517 sq. ft.; COMPLETED 1992; LOCATION San Juan Island, Washington; DESIGNER Geoffrey Prentiss (Prentiss Architects), Seattle, Washington; BUILDER Ravenhill Construction, San Juan Island, Washington; CABINETS BY Giovanni Giustina; PHOTOGRAPHER Tom Wolfe (except where noted)

TAKING ADVANTAGE OF THE fact that the structure could barely be seen from land (it's mostly hidden behind a low bank and a dense stand of lilacs), Prentiss decided to extend the camouflage by installing a sod roof. Approaching from the parking area, you're surprised to find that this seeming extension of the land out into the bay is actually a living space. And a delightful one at that.

GEOFFREY PRENTISS

RICH ZIEGNER

AS YOU SUDDENLY DISCOVER the cottage nestled behind the lilacs, a side entry welcomes you. The heavily built trellis seems to protect the building from the vastness of the site and joins the massive eave banding to indicate the strength and stability of the building.

The triangular-shaped window and sash introduce the geometry of the house before you enter.

TALL CASEMENT WINDOWS
overlooking the deck serve
as French doors, opening
the home's entire sea-facing
wall to the outdoors.

SITTING CLOSE BY THE HOUSE, the oversized trellis posts make the deck feel more intimate. From the inside of the house, the posts frame the views, reducing their potentially discomforting vastness.

Potted plants and sitting benches help extend the house into an outdoor "great" room—in every sense of the word.

INSIDE, THE DIMINUTIVE house is revealed as essentially one room: The kitchen, dining room, living room, and bedroom all share the same space.

Prentiss realized that built-in furnishings would be the key to making the most of the limited space. In addition to the kitchen cabinetry, the bed platform, headboard, storage cabinets, and bookcases—all fashioned from clear fir and pine—were custom-built for the house. (The bookcases are out of the picture.)

Except for the dining table and chairs, there is no freestanding furniture anywhere in the house.

A SINGLE ROW OF CABINETS forms a modest kitchen, providing all the storage and utilities one person could need. The refrigerator is counter-sized, hidden behind a false door and drawer face of pine plywood panels. The beams reduce in size as they approach the taller ceiling at this end of the house, increasing the perception of height.

AN ANGLED DRAWER squeezes every square inch of usable storage space out of the acute corner of this triangular-shaped house. The door pulls are hand-shaped from small branches cleared from a nearby madrone tree and set at an angle—a play on the angular motif that defines the house.

bathroom wall, revealing where the rough wall of the old pumphouse's machinery room joins the new, smooth concrete, subtly acknowledges the maritime setting of the house.

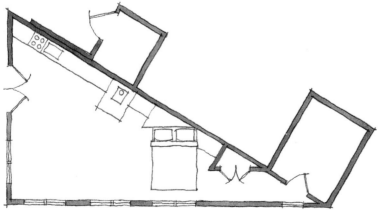

The Cottage on the Point

THE LOG CABIN on Long Point had survived nearly a century of inland squalls, but it couldn't withstand a powerful lightning strike that burned the local landmark to the ground in the summer of 1992—along with decades of summertime family memories.

Shoreline ordinances required that a new cabin be under construction within 18 months or the site would be forfeited, so the owners had to work quickly to develop a plan for its replacement. They knew they couldn't accept an off-the-shelf house design. The new summer home must not only replace the log cabin in footprint and volume (according to the ordinance) but it must also somehow recapture and renew those childhood memories for future generations. To the architect, Stephen Blatt of Portland, Maine, this meant creating a structure that looked like it had always been there—a house that felt as though it truly belonged on this special site.

SIZE 1,900 sq. ft.; COMPLETED 1994; LOCATION Long Lake, Maine; DESIGNER Stephen Blatt Architects, Portland, Maine; BUILDER Wright-Ryan Construction, Portland, Maine; PHOTOGRAPHER Brian Vanden Brink

peninsula, the multi-gabled lakeside cottage re-creates the tradition and tranquillity of a family's long-time summer cabin. The architect chose multiple, steep gables both to evoke storybook cottage imagery and to provide ample space for two second-floor bedrooms within the limited size restrictions.

To help the house blend with the barren point of rock (which had lost its stand of old-growth pines in the fire), Blatt kept the structure purposely small in scale and shaped it to rise from the promontory in graduated steps. To avoid the stark, contemporary look of broad glass surfaces, he kept the windows relatively small and used multi-paned windows on the gable ends.

the cottage on the point **61**

The challenge was to create a structure

that looked like it had always

been there—a house that felt as though it truly

belonged on this special site.

cottage along the rock-bounded, beachside trail, you enter a realm of timeless tranquillity. All is still except for the gentle rustle of the leaves and the haunting cry of the loons. The broad porch steps that wrap around the corner of the house beckon and welcome you home.

ONCE YOU REACH THE PORCH, it's hard to resist the temptation to sit awhile and enjoy the glorious view across the lake. The generous skylights—inconspicuous when viewed from outside the house because of the low pitch of the porch roof—not only brighten the porch but also bring light into the living room. The porch flooring is Port Orford cedar, chosen by the architect for its durability.

INSIDE THE HOUSE, YOU'RE immediately aware of the surprising spaciousness of the rooms. The living room is stepped down from the bright dining area, the steps defining the room as separate from the activities of the rest of the house.

The clusters of tall, narrow windows increase the sense of height and openness in the living and dining rooms and frame inviting views of the forested shoreline. Pine floors and a tall wainscot of fir bring the warmth of wood and tradition into the house, as does the huge central fireplace laid up of indigenous blue fieldstone.

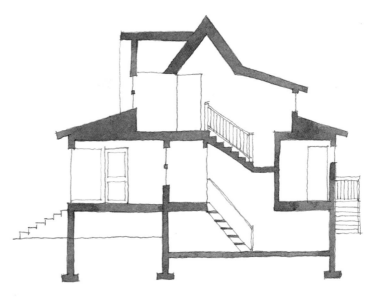

master bedroom enjoys a spectacular view across the lake to the south. The light-painted wood walls and ceiling open up the diminutive room, while built-in storage units elim-inate the need for space-consuming furniture. Wide pine board floors, exposed collar ties, and the geometric patterns of the window sash conspire to create a visually rich, memorable sleeping space.

an oval-shaped, claw-foot cast-iron tub echoes the custom-made, elegantly arched window. Painted beaded wainscot, built-in cupboards with wainscot inset panels, and a pedestal sink call to mind an earlier era.

A Playhouse by the Sea

THIS IMPRESSIVE PIECE of real estate—a point projecting into a picturesque New England cove—could not be a more auspicious place to set a vacation cottage. By the early 1920s, the owners of the site thought so too, erecting a prebuilt Hodgson house. The present trio of buildings started as one modest-sized, one-room gabled cabin; two other cabins were added alongside later.

Over the ensuing years, generations of the family would summer here, affectionately calling the diminutive waterside cottage the "Playhouse." Unfortunately, decades of rugged coastal winters took their toll, until the house fell into disrepair beyond reasonable renovation. The family realized the time had come to create a new playhouse.

The owners wanted the new structure to be reminiscent of the old one both in form and architectural detailing. But they did take advantage of the reconstruction to make essential improvements. The cottage would gather the goodness of its past as it embraced the future.

SIZE 1,718 sq. ft.; **COMPLETED** 1994; **LOCATION** Coastal Northeast; **DESIGNER** John D. Morris II Architects/Land Planners, Camden, Maine; **BUILDER** Maine Coast Construction; **PHOTOGRAPHER** Brian Vanden Brink

THE GABLED ROOMS ARE both offset from one another and angled to the waterfront, allowing each component of the house generous views of the water from at least two sides.

Thoughtful attention to architectural details helps relate the three structures to one another. For example, the arched window over the doubled-window in the living room (the center gable) is echoed by similarly curved molding over the French doors in the flanking gables.

a playhouse by the sea **67**

The cottage gathers the goodness of its past as it embraces the future.

between the house and the entrance driveway increases the cottage's sense of privacy and its role as a retreat. A restrained use of windows on this side of the house permits a preponderance of windows on the water side.

Round decorative details in each gable repeat the theme established on the waterside gables (see the photo on p. 67), and a painted horizontal banding helps unify the three gabled components of the house.

fieldstone walkway draws you to the house, the husky framing and bracket supports of the entryway's gabled roof reach out to welcome you home.

To either side of the entry, the painted band molding breaks up the flat expanse of the shingled wall. The texture of the wall is further enriched by the alternating narrow exposure of shingle courses just above the banding and by the scalloped shingles of the last courses under the roof peak.

THE MAHOGANY ENTRY DOOR, looking even broader with its flanking sidelights, glows with multiple coats of varnish. The divided light continues the four-square sash of most of the cottage's windows. Above the door, the arched lintel molding echoes the home's arched windows and gives a hint of the arched collar ties soon to be encountered in the living room.

The door to the left of the entryway leads to a closet for sailing gear. Slots cut into the door rails allow the space to breathe, letting out moisture.

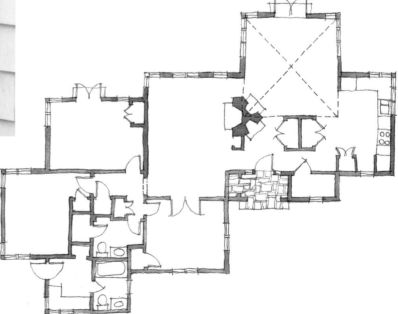

unusual feature has to be the three-sided chimney/fireplace, which was preserved from the original structure. Why have a fireplace in an entry hall? Well, just imagine you've come to this cottage on a storm-racked winter night, salt spray sharp as needles on your face: Wouldn't you be glad to be greeted by a crackling fire as you swung the door shut behind you?

IN THE LIVING ROOM, the white walls, plentiful windows, and soaring cathedral ceiling make the room feel light, airy, and spacious. The painted collar ties offer a rich and dramatic contrast to the naturally finished fir ceiling and pick up on the color theme established outside the house.

During the day, a built-in window seat by the view windows may entice you to take a nap in the sun, the sound of the harbor a murmur in the distance.

FRENCH DOORS SWING OUT
a full 180° to welcome
the outside in, while a
second set of screen doors
allows them to stay open
in bug season. To avoid
having the screens take
up valuable room in the
living space, the architect
designed them as pocket
doors so they could
slide into pockets formed
in the double-framed
exterior wall.

Corner windows in
the dining area not only
afford a magnificent view
of the harbor from the
table but also bring in
another source of light,
balancing the wealth of
light from the French-
door opening.

windows open up the room and eliminate a dark corner that would otherwise make the room feel confining. The rich tones of the wood, both on the cabinet doors and on the massive island, further help to bring richness and warmth to the space.

The island acts as a subtle boundary between the kitchen and dining room and allows the cook an unobstructed sight line to the harbor through the latter's corner window. The granite counter surface is from a local quarry.

far corner of the house, this small office with its corner window to the view, its own bathroom, and a private outside entry becomes a retreat within a retreat. The beaded wainscot carried from the wall onto the end partition of the L-shaped counter adds a welcome visual texture to the diminutive space.

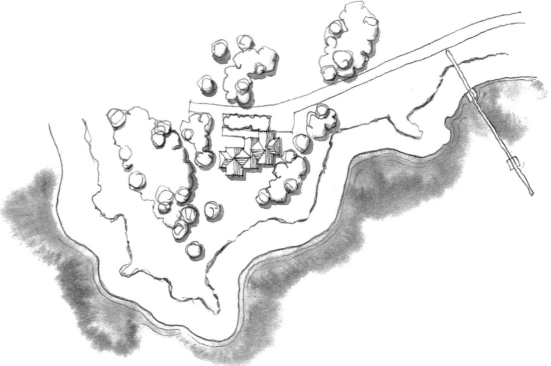

Cow Island Camp Cottage

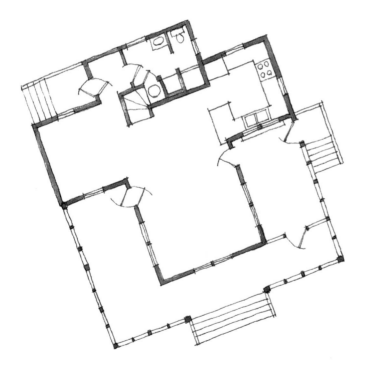

Cow Island, sitting in the middle of Lake Winnepesaukee, New Hampshire, was once a quarantine site for the Jersey cow when the animal was first imported from England. Today, it serves to "quarantine" its lucky residents from the stresses of modern life.

The owners of the cottage had come to Cow Island for years, camping on tent platforms that still sit about 100 ft. away from the house. Finding themselves wanting to spend more time here—including some winter stay-overs—they decided to create an island home for all seasons.

With no set plan in mind—other than a sense that the house must look like it belonged there—they took their architect, Rob Whitten of Portland, Maine, around the lake in a boat, pointing out lakeside cottages that had the right "feel." It soon became evident to Whitten that they were not just looking for a rustic cabin shelter but for a modest-sized house with a strong linkage to the other camp cottages surrounding the lake.

SIZE 1,775 sq. ft.; COMPLETED 1992; LOCATION Lake Winnepesaukee, New Hampshire; DESIGNER Rob Whitten and Will Winkelman (Whitten Architects); BUILDER Ken Hood, Meredith, New Hampshire; PHOTOGRAPHER Jamie Salomon

Shingle cottage style—an architecture that heavily influenced many of the camp cottages in this lake region and throughout the Northeast—Whitten gave the house broad roofs with exposed rafter ends, a wide set of entry stairs leading up to the porch, and detailing such as the turned porch columns and cross-braced rails.

Though a long way from a tent platform— and more than a rustic cabin—the simple forms, detailing, and thoughtfully chosen colors of the house tuck it in snugly amongst the island's exposed granite ledges, trees, and century-old camp cottages.

careful construction work allowed the cottage to nestle closely between the trees and rock outcroppings. The screened-in porch provides outdoor dining space in the buggy spring season, while the rest of the porch remains open. Vertical battens over the crawl space are a welcome relief from the ubiquitous store-bought garden panels of crosshatched thin cedar strips.

The red-painted door and window frames enliven what might otherwise have been a rather bland field of brown siding. While old-style casement windows tuck under the eave of the roof, on the gable-end wall doublehung windows set directly in line with each other (as they are on the front gable) build upon the overall symmetry of the house.

plan and 9-ft. ceiling expand the sense of spaciousness, the prominent hearth flanked by tree posts cut from the site, red-pine floors and white-pine paneling, and the exposed interior framing give back a sense of warmth and coziness.

To the right of the fireplace a counter projects out from the kitchen to provide an informal dining area. The sit-down dining room is reached through the hall that runs behind the fireplace. At the entrance to the kitchen, the built-in pantry almost disappears into the beaded wallboard paneling when its doors are closed.

fireplace—the hall that
connects the kitchen to
the dining room—is,
according to its architect,
the "white space" of the
house. Though not a room
in itself, it becomes what-
ever it finds itself used
for: a transition space for

the back entrance of the
house (which contains a
bathroom and shower),
access to the dining table,
or a warm, informal space
for the kids to hang out in
while mom and dad are
fixing dinner.

AS YOU STAND AT THE TOP of the stairs, your eye is drawn through the hallway into the master bedroom and then out to a lovely view of the lake beyond. The vertical line of masonry graciously serves to break up an otherwise monotonous surface of pine paneling—which, if you look carefully, camouflages a hall closet.

The passage door's transom window encourages heated air from the first floor's wood stove or fireplace to flow into the bedroom. Sparse, simply styled furnishings and lighting fixtures increase both the sense of spaciousness and the modest simplicity of this lakeside camp cottage.

Cottage Cluster East

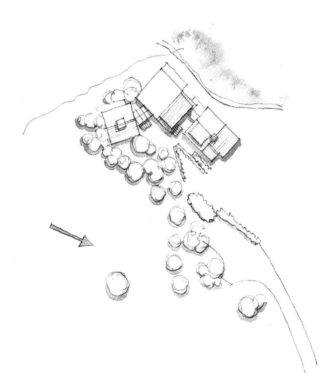

THIS ENCHANTING CLUSTER of cottages started out as a single 1960s-era two-story residence sitting within a patch of thick woods on a site that sloped gently and enticingly to the sea. Ripe for remodel, the existing house offered an anchor for the two new structures, allowing them to be built dramatically close to the sea's high-water mark.

In the design of the remodel and expansion, the clients had a clear idea of what they *didn't* want: a neat-as-a-pin, classically symmetrical, and "proper" looking house—the kind of home they lived in throughout most of the year. Instead, they wanted this coastal cluster of cottage forms to afford, through its whimsical details and exuberant land-scaping, a welcome retreat from their more urbane wintertime lifestyle. At the same time, the owners challenged the architects to create a balanced, inte-grated composition. As you will see, they succeeded.

SIZE 3,200 sq. ft. (total of three buildings); COMPLETED 1996; LOCATION Maine coast; DESIGNER Richard Bernhard and John Priestley, Architects, Rockport, Maine; LANDSCAPE ARCHITECT Karen Kettlety, Mt. Desert, Maine; BUILDER Bay Design and Construction; PHOTOGRAPHER Brian Vanden Brink

THE ARCHITECTS CREATED
three separate buildings, each carefully oriented to one another to afford privacy and also angled to follow the shoreline to gain maximum sun and view exposure. The cottage bearing the arched entry trellis is the main house— the original structure. The guest lodge sits to the right. In winter, this structure can operate independently of the main house as a cozy, easy-to-heat retreat. To the left, just out of the picture (you can see its glassed-in breezeway), lies the master-bedroom annex.

THE CHARMING ARBOR entryway to the kitchen (left) achieves a sense of rustic refinement through its turned newel posts, curved side rails, and hand-laid lattice work. Attention to details doesn't stop here: The painted horizontal trim banding and the narrow courses added between each course of shingles at the first-floor wall differentiate the floors, reducing an otherwise monolithic two-story wall of shingles.

The clustered cottages are surrounded by almost wild-feeling, exuberantly colored flower gardens, rather than by the more traditional formal gardens and lawn.

THE USE OF A BREEZEWAY
to connect the guest lodge
with the main house pro-
vides a comfortable degree
of separation between
hosts and guests. The sense
of separation can be made
more distinct if the French
doors to either side are
left open to allow the sea
breeze to sweep through.

Wicker furniture and
flower boxes create an inviting deck space or, when
moved into the breezeway,
a sheltered outside room.

cottage complex, reached by a long path through the forest and flower gardens, links the main house and the master-bedroom annex. Seen through the glazed doors on either side of the breezeway, the space becomes transparent, allowing the green moss of the foreground and the water view beyond to draw you to the house.

The choice of rustic, log-style detailing differentiates this breezeway from that connecting the main house and the guest lodge and represents a conscious diversion from symmetry as well as a sense of playfulness and charm. Coming to this entry, the owners know they are a long way from the neoclassic house they left behind in the suburbs.

THE MAIN-HOUSE DECK, wide enough to accommodate a congenial circle of chairs, offers a sweeping view of the water and islands. The native fieldstone wall is the back of the living-room fireplace.

The owners have tastefully chosen to furnish the deck with old painted rockers instead of the generic plastic chairs that have invaded so many seaside decks.

lodge, in contrast to the main-house deck, is intimate, opening directly off the bedroom and offering a private outside space that can't be seen from (and can't see over to) the main house. The swing-out windows in the background enthusiastically open the sitting room of the lodge to the ocean views and aromas.

A WINDING FLAGSTONE PATH leads through the "white garden" to the master-bedroom annex. As planned by the landscape architect, "Fragrant flowers such as Clethra and oriental lilies add to the sensory experience of this evening garden." The predominantly white blossoms and variegated foliage—glowing in the subtle downlights that mimic moonlight—are reflected in the bedroom's white bedding and natural-colored area rug.

The glass-roofed monitor atop the bedroom gathers light and allows star gazing, while the broad glazing draws in the forest and ocean views to the rustic bed set against the far wall.

BECAUSE THE ROOF OF THE master-bedroom annex is overlaid with rigid insulation, the rafters and wood sheathing can be exposed to view, making the space feel rustic and snug—even with the vast expanses of glass (most of which slide open). The wooden slat shades blend unobtrusively into the wall structure, fully out of the way when you wish the view to enter the room.

the owners was that these cottages, though small in scale, would offer an open, expansive feeling from within. The architects strove to ensure this by providing expansive windows and numerous doors—many French doubles—between rooms and to the outside. In this living room, huge, swing-out windows bring the outside in.

Above, a long eyebrow window gracefully sweeps across the second-story wall. At the same time, the stone fireplace, the rich wood tones of the wall and ceiling, the wicker furnishings, and the floral colored fabrics maintain the rustic coziness of the space.

room, a built-in library unit surrounds the breeze-way door. To ensure that the large-scale built-in would blend harmoniously into the small room, the architects carefully propor-tioned and aligned its trimwork: The library's rail and stile work is sized to match the casement trim around the room's doors and windows. Also, the top frieze board continues as a banding around the room, separating the verti-cally laid paneling from the wall boards above.

A COZY READING ALCOVE

in the guest-lodge sitting room faces a matching alcove set into the garden wall. The alcove doubles as sleeping space when there are more beds than guests. Its cathedral ceiling lends the space an almost chapel-like quality: spaciousness in spirit, yet snug and serene.

The bookcase set into the wall maximizes the use of the space, as do the generous storage areas for bedding provided under the cushions. Again, notice that the trim of the built-in matches that of the window trim. The wall banding above becomes the bottom trim of the upper windows, bringing these elements into a comfortable visual harmony.

Cottages

of the Forest and Mountains

A well-worn path winding through the
sun-dappled woods, a whiff of woodsmoke
carried on the rustling wind, a hint of
amber light shining between
a stand of trees—and suddenly you are
there, drawn within the warm embrace
of your forest cottage home.

At Home on the Forest Trail

F INDING THE RIGHT SITE for a house is probably the most important decision to be made in the design process. The owner of this cottage lived for several years in a small, temporary cabin on a corner of the property and spent much time wandering through its fields and trails looking for a building site for the permanent house. While many sites came to mind, none ever felt just right to her. Finally, nearly at the point of giving up, she realized she had "known" the spot all along: a beautiful grove of fir trees on a knoll upon which she would often come to meditate.

The diminutive cottage nestles snugly amongst the trees and straddles the original forest trail. With the entry placed directly along the path—as are the French doors to the back of the house—you get the sense that the trail leads not just to the house, but continues through it and into the forest beyond. Rather than occupying the original forest path and meditation spot, this home has, for the owner, become it.

SIZE 850 sq. ft.; COMPLETED 1989; LOCATION Whidbey Island, Washington; DESIGNER Ross Chapin, Langley, Washington; BUILDER Kim Hoelting; PHOTOGRAPHER Craig Wester

of tall fir trees, a cascade of gables embraces the house, evoking the feeling of a wayside forest chapel. The first gable shelters a welcoming porch, the second gable the entry room, bathroom, and laundry, and the third gable steps up to enclose the main living space of the house, including two upstairs bedrooms and a bathroom. The high pitch and generous overhangs of the roof eaves bring them within reach, scaling down the house to comforting human proportions.

the house appears to rise up out of the green-carpeted forest floor. French doors opening to porches on both floors encourage you to enter the forest, even on rainy evenings. The roof's wide side eaves and gable over-hangs help keep rain water off the walls and well out-side the porches.

Look closely at the tall porch posts on both floors: Vertically aligned to one another, they echo the tall, thin fir trees surrounding the cottage. Rough-hewn porch rails and balusters acknowledge the primeval forest setting.

AS YOU COME INSIDE

the house, the first thing that strikes you is the variation in ceiling heights. The low ceiling at the entry gives way to a higher open-beam ceiling in the kitchen/dining room (shown at left and above), dropping again to a lower ceiling in the living room. These changes in height cause a sense of compression and release as you move through the cottage, accentuating an illusion of spaciousness in the main living space.

Overhead, a shelf supporting a line of books appears to act as a decorative header.

tiny kitchen maximizes efficiency in such a small space and creates both a buffer and a serving table to the dining area. Directly over the sink counter area, skylights set into the ceiling (which extends up past the second floor) flood the counter and hanging plants atop the perimeter shelf with an abundance of morning light. The brightly painted china cabinet adds a cheerful splash of color to the predominantly wood-toned interior.

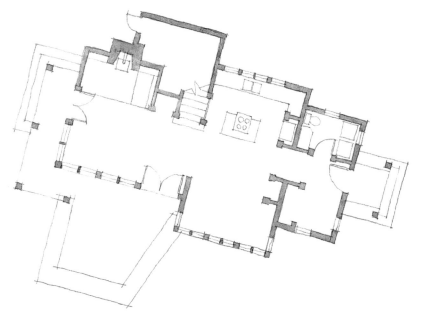

IN THE LIVING ROOM,

an inglenook raised above the wood floor on a broad brick hearth creates a warm, intimate space for reading and napping by the Rumford-style fireplace—now occupied by a more efficient wood stove. The massive chimney tapers smaller as it rises from its base, a design strategy that lends the chimney a sense of stability and grace.

IN A SMALL COTTAGE,

the clever use of space can add functional areas without creating clutter or intruding on the primary living areas. Here, a daybed set on a stairway landing makes use of an otherwise little-used space. Kids old enough to handle stairs well find this to be an ideal playspace—out of the way yet close by the action.

With the curtains pulled, this space can provide a miniature bedroom for guests (at least those not prone to sleepwalking!). Bedding stores conveniently below the mattress platform.

THE TWO-STORY, SHED-TYPE structure, a marked contrast to the gable end, contains a kitchen on the first level and a sleeping space on the second. The shed steps up from the southern portion of the house to accommodate the slope of the site.

To keep costs down, the chimney pipe is enclosed by a framed box covered with cedar shingles—left natural to contrast with the painted cedar clapboards. The trim on the west wall ties the windows of both floor levels together, a design strategy that gives visual pleasure and coherence to what might otherwise be a disjointed (and uninteresting) wall face.

A HUGE FIREPLACE LAID UP of local fieldstones graces one wall of the great room, easily heating the house in the fall and spring. The mason supported the mantel shelf—a massive plank of old-growth chestnut—by inlaying a portion of it into the stones. The Mexican tile floor acts as a heat sink after absorbing warmth from the sun throughout the day.

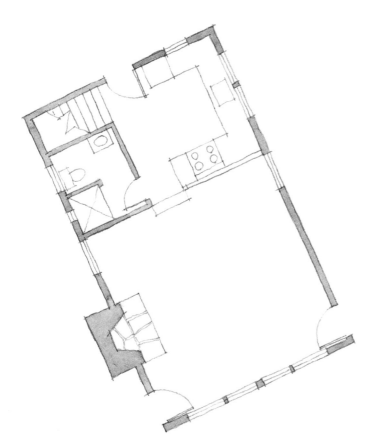

SINCE THE SHED STEPS UP the slope behind the great room, the kitchen is necessarily a couple of steps higher. This is not a design quirk without purpose: The raised kitchen floor helps define the space and its functions as being separate, though not divorced, from those of the living room. Also, the higher perch allows the cook to see over the people and furnishings of the great room and into the forest beyond.

A triangular cutout at the peak of the partition between the two structures provides a lookout from the loft.

A Twin-Gabled Forest Cottage

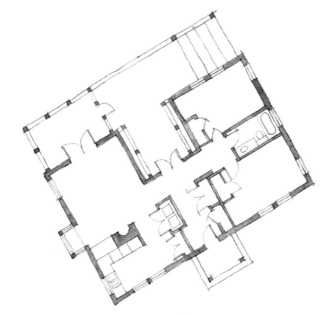

S HELTERED IN A DENSE HARDWOOD forest, this twin-gabled dwelling evokes the spirit of the cozy "camp cottages" built of stone and shingle throughout New England since the middle of the last century. The house is compact, warm, and rich with indigenous materials, making you feel protected and snug at home in the wild forest setting. Yet generous windows, an alluring window seat, a set of French doors, and an expansive deck conspire to draw you outdoors.

To afford the functions of both privacy and society within such a modest footprint, architect Jim Sterling set two bedrooms and a bathroom under one gable, a living room and kitchen under the other, and a hall and entry foyer in between. You can walk right through the cottage from the entry door to the deck without disturbing a soul.

SIZE 1,100 sq. ft.; COMPLETED 1990; LOCATION Naples, Maine; DESIGNER Jim Sterling, Architect, Portland, Maine; BUILDER Sewall Associates, Portland, Maine; PHOTOGRAPHER Brian Vanden Brink (except where noted)

THOUGHTFUL SITE ORIENTATION and careful workmanship during the construction phase minimized tree removal, allowing the cottage to nestle close into the surrounding oak and maple forest. Around the house and along trails cut through the forest to a lake, the owners planted low-maintenance, shade-loving plants—in just a year or two, the cottage looked as if it had been on the site for a century.

...snug at home in a wild forest setting

materials and colors blends the house seamlessly into the surrounding forest: naturally finished cedar shingle siding, forest-green trim and gable siding, slate-gray composition roof, and a chimney laid up of local fieldstone. The tiny cross-gable caps the living room's window seat punch-out, a room-within-a-room that has tall windows on three sides to draw the forest (and its dappled light) into the house.

JAMIE SALOMON

THE PORCH'S PAINTED
interior and tightly laid hardwood floor give the room a sense of formality, decidedly linking it to the interior living spaces. At the same time, wicker furnishings, an old pine wood drop-leaf table that serves as a dining table for two, and an abundance of potted plants assert a forest camp ambiance.

THE SCREENED-IN PORCH
and expansive deck face the lake and the trail to the dock. For three seasons, these two spaces are central to the outdoor life of the cottage.

The angled caps on the railing posts not only reflect the gables of the house but also have a practical aspect: They shed the rain, snow, and tree detritus that often leads to rot if captured on flat wood surfaces or joints. The horizontal sections of the railings are rounded to achieve the same purpose—and to feel soft to the touch.

a twin-gabled forest cottage **109**

through a granite-faced
tower of masonry that
centers on the peak of the
cathedral ceiling; its strong
vertical thrust initiates a
sense of spaciousness
in this deceptively large-
feeling great room. The
space also expands visually
through an abundance
of light refraction from
white-painted walls,
pickled-white cedar ceiling
boards, and light-colored
wood floors.

At the far end of the
room, a window placed high
on the gable wall opens
out, casement style, to
cool the house on muggy
summer days. Below, a
tiny, efficient kitchen and
dining area tucks behind
the fireplace.

THE WINDOW SEAT, ITS TRIO of tall windows framing the slender tree trunks beyond, is bathed in light, even in winter months. This is obviously a well-used, well-loved corner of the cottage.

FOR MANY YEARS, the owners of this striking mountainside home on Orcas Island had shared a passion for the art and architecture of provincial France. Avid collectors of Provençal furnishings and crafts, they had long planned to build a modest-sized house that would give their collection—and their dreams—a fitting home. Working with architect Jack Jackson, they came up with a vision: a 19th-century French hunting lodge framed with disproportionately large timbers and replete with mansard roof, copper-covered turret, quoins, and dormers. Their intent was to create a house that would have looked and felt at home amongst the Provençal cottages of the last century.

A French Hunting Lodge in the Pacific Northwest

SIZE 1,940 sq. ft.; COMPLETED 1988; LOCATION Orcas Island, Washington; DESIGNER Jack Jackson, Orcas Island, Washington; BUILDER Dave Shore; PHOTOGRAPHER Craig Wester

roof is penetrated by
arched, gabled, and bayed
windows, which offer a
panoramic view of the
San Juan Islands. Quoins
at the wall corners and
the bright blue entry door
are typical of Provençal
cottages.

The thick eave boards,
stepped out to create
shadow lines, appear to
support and graduate the
bottom of the house with
the huge roof.

THE ARCHITECT CREATED

a bright, luminous interior by using relatively big windows, which draw the light in and make the most of the view. At the same time, the ceilings made low by oversized joist timbers, a large wood stove on a raised hearth, and cheerful colors in the decor give a sense of warmth and coziness.

THE U-SHAPED KITCHEN

opens to the living room, separated only by a breakfast bar. Just a step away, the dining area sits in a bay window filled with flowers. The tiles on the countertop, made in Portugal to a French Provençal pattern, carry over to the dining table.

Adhering to tradition, the kitchen cabinets feature full-recess doors, glazed upper cabinets, and brass knobs.

that form the structure of the house are joined entirely with wood-to-wood joints—mostly pinned mortise and tenons. The inward lean of the roof made the joinery particularly challenging for the framers. The solid knee braces add a bit more shear resistance and mass to the framework.

IN THE UPSTAIRS MASTER bedroom, a huge window runs from the floor to the top of the arched dormer cut into the mansard roof. Though the substantial sash moldings give some sense of security, you almost feel as though you could fly forth across the forested hills to the sea beyond. A sleeping loft, its edge curved to echo the arched window frame, fully exploits the room's tall ceiling.

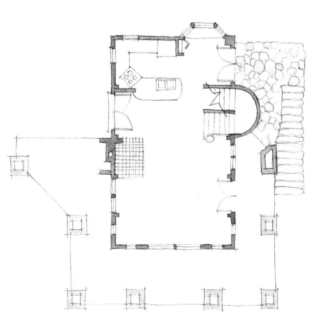

LOG CABINS ARE LOG CABINS, cottages are cottages, and never the twain shall meet. At least that's what I thought until I came upon this small log house in the Maine woods. The expansive,

A Cottage Made of Logs

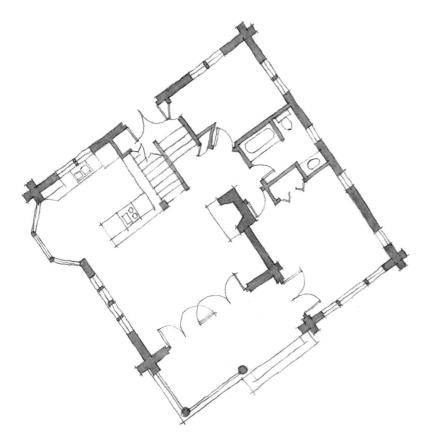

high-pitched, cross-gabled roof with its generous overhangs was the first clue that this was not your typical Wild West cabin. Looking closer, I found myself drawn to numerous, delightful details: gracefully arched structural timbers and windows, unique decorative twig and trim work, and careful landscaping that smoothly ties the house to its sloped site. All these attributes say "cottage" loud and clear.

SIZE 1,296 sq. ft.; COMPLETED 1994; LOCATION Naples, Maine; DESIGNER Timothy and Elizabeth Bullock, Creemore, Ontario, Canada; BUILDER Bullock and Company, Ontario, Canada; PHOTOGRAPHER Brian Vanden Brink

with a combination of stacked logs and framed timbers. Designers Timothy and Elizabeth Bullock selected the logs to suit the scale of the house, peeled them of their bark, and then shaped them to fit tightly against one another. Massive saddle-notches at the corners join the walls together. The roof is framed of heavy pine timbers, joined primarily with pinned mortise and tenons.

house, complementing the primary gable, a smaller, less steeply pitched gable defines the master bedroom and protects the log walls from direct rain. Both gables shelter a window wall pierced through with timbers; each features curved timbers arching out from the centerline of the gable to support the roof.

The logs are cut sequentially to create a curved "bracket" under the smaller gable's roof eave. A turned pin hangs from the peak, providing a decorative juncture for the otherwise plain bargeboards.

AT THE CORNERS OF THE house, the alternating sizes of the logs are clearly revealed. The more typical log cabin of uniformly sized logs is far less interesting visually. The hand-chamfered edges at the log ends attest to the builder's close attention to detail. The decorative twig work brings down the scale of the log work while helping to define the facets of the kitchen's bay window.

THE SCREENED-IN PORCH provides a welcome retreat on buggy summer evenings. The designers maintained the stepped effect of the logs on the porch, even though the protrusions made it more difficult to fit the screening. The narrow, tongue-and-groove pine ceiling boards and wrought-copper light fixtures are in keeping with the cottage-like style of the house.

THE GREAT ROOM IS A
resounding symphony of
wood: naturally finished
log walls, vertical paneling,
ceiling boards, and an
intricate, exposed post-
and-beam framing system,
which is echoed by the
gable-end window framing.

Crafted in similar wood
and style, the stairs and
balcony meld with the
home's structural frame-
work. A raised-counter bar
separates the kitchen area
without closing it off
from family activities in
the great room.

IN THE KID'S BEDROOM
(above), a bunk built over
the closet and reached by
a ship's ladder provides an
extra berth for sleepovers.
Beaded pine boards panel
the walls, running vertically
to add a sense of height.

Left: In the master bedroom, a "defect" in a
log becomes a shelf for
watches and rings at the
head of the bed.

ARCHITECT JOHN CAMPBELL of Orcas Island, Washington, decided that if he was going to build a house "on spec," it would have to be a house he could feel proud to attach his name to. Campbell decided to articulate the design with the island's predominant 1920s' camp-cottage architecture close in mind. Not only would this keep the neighbors happy, but the simple (and small) traditional shape would help keep costs down. He was happy to spend the savings of money and energy on details that would give this island cottage in the woods vitality and a unique charm.

To make the most of the small footprint, Campbell made the house a tall one-and-a-half

An Island Cottage on Spec

stories, creating 9-ft. ceilings on the first floor to imbue the first-level rooms with a feeling of spaciousness and to create usable bedrooms on the second floor.

SIZE 1,296 sq. ft.; COMPLETED 1994; LOCATION Orcas Island, Washington; DESIGNER John M. Campbell (Architect), Orcas Island, Washington; BUILDER John M. Campbell; PHOTOGRAPHER Michael Skott

THE CHIMNEY WAS LAID UP by mason Joseph Kinney from local glacial till. Its chimney-pot-style flue cap is a traditional cottage design element. The out-look-style bargeboards, supported by rather hefty knee brackets, lend an expressive detail that helps link the house to other traditional island homes.

The steeply pitched shed roof over the porch protects the French doors facing the view. Notice the second horizontal trim detail on the porch rail—a thoughtful addition that gives the balustrade more substance and visual appeal.

room blazes within the stone fireplace capped with a custom-made mantelpiece of local Douglas fir. The high ceiling, enlivened with closely spaced floor joists, is painted white to reflect light and to reduce shadows between the joists. The white-painted French doors open to the front, south-facing deck. Clear fir trimwork runs throughout the cottage.

as open as possible, only a half-wall separates the kitchen from the dining area. Light-colored, simply designed wood furnishings add to the sense of spaciousness. Red-oak kitchen cabinets pick up on the oak flooring running throughout the rest of the house.

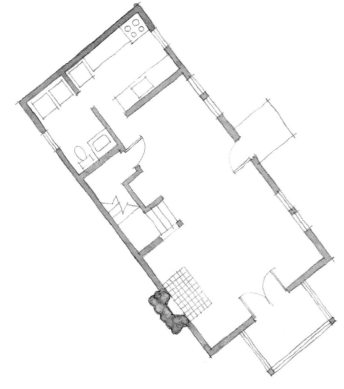

GENEROUS WEST-FACING
windows bring plenty of light into the upstairs master bedroom. The unusual ceiling angles, which relieve any chance of lay-a-bed boredom, are created by the gabled dormer as it embraces the outside chimney.

THE OWNER OF THIS NEW ISLAND HOME in the woods had lived for years in a rambling house in the city, and she wanted her retirement house to have a similar feel and function. Like the old

A Cottage Cluster in the Woods

house, this one must allow her to move from room to room to suit the light of day and her moods and activities of the moment.

The designers came up with the idea of creating a cluster of three simple cottages joined by long hallways. Paying close attention to the sun's path, they laid out the three units so the bedroom faces east to start the owner's day with the dawn; the great room and kitchen sit squarely in the middle; while the library sits quietly to the west, offering a cozy farewell to the sun.

SIZE 2,250 sq. ft.; COMPLETED 1996; LOCATION San Juan Island, Washington; DESIGNERS Peter Kilpatrick and Jeanne Mitchell Lee, Friday Harbor, Washington; Brad Burgess, Seattle, Washington; BUILDER Ravenhill Construction, Friday Harbor, Washington; PHOTOGRAPHER Craig Wester

at an angle and parallel to one another—and then inserting the main entry cubical at its own angle— the designers created some interesting spatial relationships to entertain the eye. But more than that, the positioning also allowed them to bring unencumbered views and sunshine into the ends and side decks of the bedroom and living room. No matter which unit you find yourself in, you are given a place to enjoy the exceptional siting of this house.

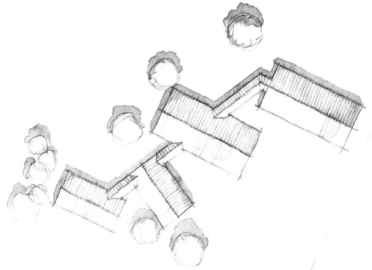

a cottage cluster in the woods **127**

great room, a cathedral ceiling—reinforced by light-colored walls and warm wood tones—gives the relatively narrow room a feeling of expansiveness and light. A peak-straddling skylight floods the room with natural light to illuminate and enliven daytime activities.

The partition wall to the rear, fitted with leaded lights, separates the entryway/pantry area without blocking light or the view into the trees. The naturally finished wood floor is larch.

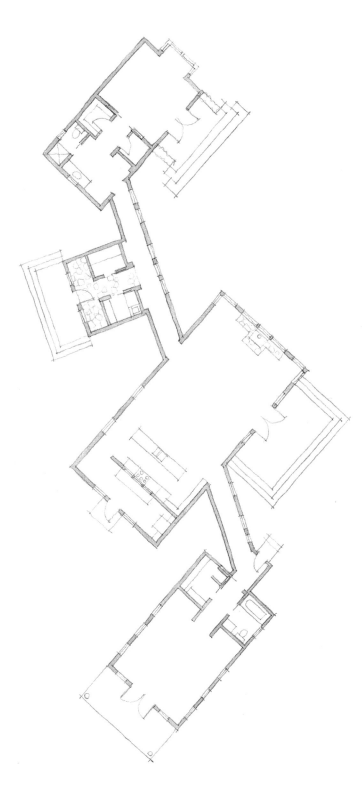

AT THE END OF THE KITCHEN, just a step away from the food-prep counters and stove, open shelving with beaded-panel backs fills the wall. The sandstone countertops to the left and right lend a rich, variegated color to the space.

TALL, NARROW WINDOWS maintain a sense of coziness while alleviating a potential sense of confinement within this relatively tiny sitting room/library. The strong vertical views draw your eye both to the ground and to the trees, reinforcing your awareness of the home's wooded surroundings.

THIS DAYBED TUCKED INTO an alcove in the sitting room/library is perfectly situated for an afternoon nap as the sun bathes the western face of the cottage in soft afternoon light. A second alcove sits in the other corner at this end of the room. Built-in bookshelves and storage cabinets line the north wall of the room.

TO ACCOMMODATE THE owner's antique desk while offering a lovely view through the forest to the bay beyond, the designers pushed out the wall of the master bedroom, lining it with windows. Facing due east, the alcove welcomes the first light of day and encourages morning correspondence.

TO SIMPLIFY CONSTRUCTION and to reinforce contemporary design elements, Prentiss eliminated traditional trimwork around windows and door openings. The strong vertical proportions reinforced by the pole mullions and dramatic color combinations avoid the featureless, blank stare of modern picture windows.

The unheated vestibule on the side porch offers a weather barrier for the entryway while also providing a coat closet and a pantry area for the kitchen that does not encroach upon the precious 600-sq.-ft. footprint.

THE PAINTED STEEL POLES have come inside to support the sleeping and storage loft. Smaller versions of the posts form balusters, while cable guardrails allow an unobstructed view of the mountains through the windows in the south gable. Below the loft, an island defines the boundary between the kitchen and dining area.

A BUILT-IN WINDOW SEAT mirroring the one in the dining area runs the full length of the living room's side wall, adding color, comfort, and economy of space.

To add a pleasing texture and to differentiate some of the wall surfaces, Prentiss specified the installation of horizontal beaded paneling in the living room.

THE FIRST-FLOOR BEDROOMS
are designed as mirror images, down to the identical built-in bed platforms, headboards, and bookshelves (only the books are different). Clothing and bedding drawers slide out on rollers from under the bed platforms to maximize storage potential.

A short partition-wall alcove to the right of the bedroom doorway is fitted with built-in shelving to create a bookcase. Throughout the cottage, finely crafted built-in furnishings make the most of the limited space while adding a good measure of charm.

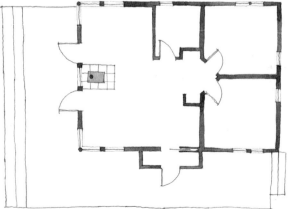

A SHIP'S-TYPE LADDER
(with painted metal handrails to continue the theme of the steel columns) provides access to the sleeping loft, eliminating the need for a space-consuming stairway.

Right: Soaring gable windows and a welcome absence of clutter create an open, airy space—like the fields and mountains upon which this cottage will gaze for many generations.

a little house for a big mountain **139**

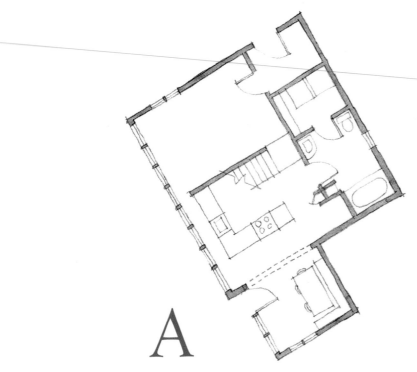

A Modest Cottage on the Vineyard

HERE'S A CHALLENGE: Build a two-bedroom, passive-solar-heated house—including all design and sitework—within the economic restraints of a modest FHA low-interest loan. And, yes, make the house both uniquely attractive and cozy and true to the architectural heritage of the region.

To meet this double-edged challenge, South Mountain Company of Chilmark, Massachusetts, worked with the owner to keep the floor plan as small and simple as possible. The budget allowed some quality workmanship and materials—not to mention a measure of quirkiness—to enter the picture: tiled floors, substantial trimwork, built-ins tucked into nooks and crannies, leaded-glass inserts in some windows, and cedar clapboards.

To make the house cozy in the most economical way possible, large glazed windows face due south, allowing the masonry floor and an interior brick wall to gather and hold heat. Though this house was kept extraordinarily modest in size, it became filled with a huge sense of place and belonging.

SIZE 900 sq. ft.; COMPLETED 1980; LOCATION Martha's Vineyard, Massachusetts; DESIGNER/BUILDER South Mountain Company, Chilmark, Massachusetts; PHOTOGRAPHER John Abrams

TO REDUCE OVERHEATING during the summer months, the owner covered the large south-facing windows with a trellis overrun with a riot of morning glories. Tall, narrow windows with leaded sash, substantial eave moldings, and tightly set clapboards speak of quality and lend the house a certain dignity. The clapboards were left natural not only to reduce maintenance costs but also to recognize the architectural tradition of Martha's Vineyard.

along both outside walls of the dining room frame and echo the form of the tree trunks at the property boundary. Because the windows reach close to the floor, even when seated you can see the lawn, drawing its beauty and rich light into the room.

Built-in benches along the inside wall maximize the use of space, while the cathedral ceiling opens up the room and enlivens the interior landscape of the house.

SUMMER SUNLIGHT FILTERED through the vines softens the light flowing into the house while keeping the air and objects inside the house cool and comfortable. In the winter, the absence of leaves allows the full light of the sun to heat the bricks and tiles. The twine trellis centers on the window openings to increase the sense of verticality and visual interest.

SOLID-WOOD COUNTERS SET over white-painted wood cabinets featuring full-inset frame-and-panel doors recall traditional kitchen cabinetry of the region. A raised ledge by the window—perfect for holding plants and decorative objects—provides a backstop for the counter.

Built-in shelving and storage cupboards under the stairs take full advantage of this quirky space. The stair stringer, left as natural wood, provides a pleasing backdrop for the owner's plate collection as well as a handy surface to hang herbs and potholders.

Island Cottage in Stone

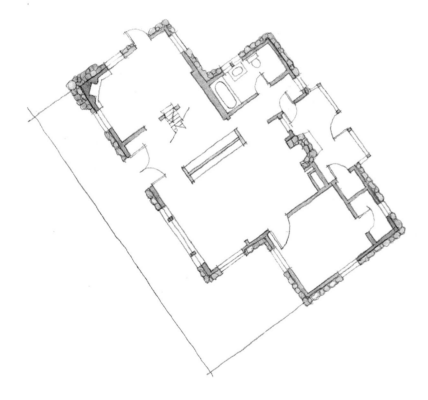

THIS ISLAND COTTAGE is a complete renovation of a 1920s' stone and cedar-shingle farmhouse set on an open pasture that slopes to a south-facing bay off Puget Sound. Though the exterior stone walls were retained, an infestation of beetles demanded that all the wood structures be replaced.

On the outside, the designers carefully maintained the traditional appearance, letting the original stone structure dictate the placement of doors and windows. They treated the inside, however, to innovative and contemporary design solutions: The kitchen was opened to the dining room with its ocean views, a playloft was added above the kitchen, and all surfaces were made smooth and cleanly finished. The goal was to create a relaxing, picturesque house that acknowledges its island history without forsaking the needs and aesthetics of the present.

SIZE 1,365 sq. ft.; COMPLETED 1995; LOCATION Lopez Island, Washington; DESIGNER Olson Sundberg Architects, Seattle, Washington; BUILDER Dan Harris; PHOTOGRAPHER Michael Skott

AN ANGLED ROOF OVERHANG, reminiscent of 19th-century cottage designs, shelters the walls and windows under the centered cross-gable. The large windows are broken up by solid wood sash to reduce their otherwise monolithic scale and to help frame the views from inside the house. A smaller cross-gable, just visible behind the larger one, defines and dignifies the entryway.

...a relaxing, picturesque house that acknowledges its island history without forsaking the needs and aesthetics of the present.

THIS SIDE OF THE HOUSE was purposefully designed to blend with the land-scape—to make it appear to emerge from the field of wild grasses. A heavily built trellis creates an out-door eating area reached by a Dutch door leading from the dining room. The massive old stone chimney visually anchors the corner of the building.

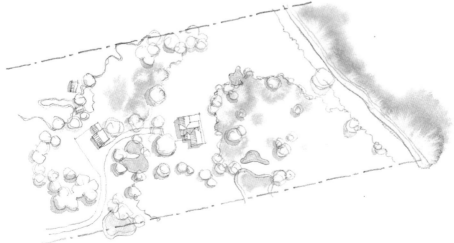

THE EXISTING PORCH was glazed in to create a protected foyer, which lights up like a lamp at dusk, offering a warm and inviting welcome. The graceful lines of the old farmhouse are particularly evident in this view.

and steel collar ties lighten the feeling inside the house, in contrast to the heavy masses of the exterior. Custom-made built-in bookcases line the living-room wall. The floor is stained concrete.

AN UNDERSTATED FIREPLACE maintains the smooth, clean lines of the cottage interior, while horizontal beaded panels on the walls provide a textural contrast.

THE BUILT-IN LADDER, gracefully framed with waxed steel rails that relate visually to the collar ties, leads up to the playloft over the kitchen. In the kitchen, the clear-finished plywood casework features integral pulls that expose the cabinet's interior partitions. This trick adds much visual interest to the otherwise monolithic surfaces.

Stone Cottage Revival

© NORMAN McGRATH

THE HOUSE WAS ALMOST not worth saving. Rot had permeated most of the wooden roof and wall framing, but the owners saw the potential for reviving this classic stone cottage and hired Centerbrook Architects of Essex, Connecticut, to restore the house from the inside out.

Following the advice of the contractor, the building was stripped down to its stone walls and some of the roof and floor structure. Then the restoration work began in earnest: Through the hands of many talented craftsmen, the architects regenerated the essence of the old cottage by reintroducing new windows, doors, paneling, casework, and flooring in traditional styling and materials. While some charms of the home's earlier life were left intact—the exposed chimney structure and quirky tiny "room" spaces, for example—expanded open volumes and light-toned surfaces encouraged the house to meet contemporary living sensibilities.

SIZE 1,900 sq. ft.; COMPLETED 1985; LOCATION Dutchess County, New York; DESIGNER Centerbrook Architects, Essex, Connecticut; PHOTOGRAPHER Norman McGrath

SITTING AT THE EDGE OF a rolling green meadow and tucked into a stand of hardwood trees, the restored cottage looks much as it did in the last century. Only the skylights (visible in the photo on the facing page) denote a concession to a modern cottage lifestyle.

THE DARK, THICKLY PAINTED wall panels and ceiling (all made of solid wood) lend a sense of formality to the space around the traditional walk-in fire-place. At the same time, the heavy exposed joist beams and the stuffed upholstered furniture make the space feel cozy and intimate.

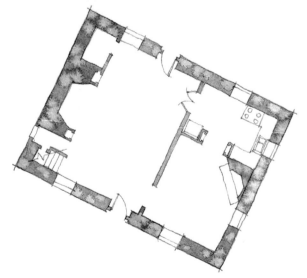

IN THIS PART OF THE GREAT
room, the exposed beams are left rough and unpainted—giving the room an almost primitive feeling. The white-painted, stuccoed chimney, as well as the wall surfaces, bring light and a feeling of spaciousness to an otherwise dark corner of the house. The steep stairs, a survival of the house's past, climb to the upstairs bedrooms.

© NORMAN McGRATH

© NORMAN McGRATH

THE BATTENED, WIDE-PLANK double doors open butler style to reveal a traditional-looking kitchen featuring painted wood cabinets with raised-panel doors.

The open shelves and herbs hanging from the exposed floor joists evoke the imagery of an old-style dry-goods pantry space.

THE SENSE OF SOLIDITY and genuineness of this old stone cottage is nowhere more evident than in the traditional dining-room setting. Sitting at the table by a warm fire, diners are surrounded by heavy ceiling timbers, flooring of old pine boards, painted horizontal-board wainscot, and walls penetrated by deep recesses surrounding the windows. Because of the small amount of natural light admitted to the room, the walls and ceiling are painted a light color.

THIS QUIRKY, ODD-SHAPED space tucked under an upstairs eave serves as a quiet, intimate spot for writing correspondence. It also draws you back to the pre-restoration life of this home, where similar spaces made use of every nook and cranny.

Salvage-Yard Vernacular

TYPICALLY, THE COTTAGE is a house composed of, and surrounded by, wood and stone. These are the indigenous materials that have always inhabited the visual and structural landscape of these small vernacular homes. But this small house, designed by Dan Rockhill of Lecompton, Kansas, pushes the notion of "indigenous" to include the materials of another American vernacularism: the salvage yard.

When Rockhill's clients approached him with the idea of building a home for their family within the seemingly impossible budget of $50,000, he realized that he would have to build with what was most readily (and thus most cheaply) available. A trip to the salvage yard netted 30-ft.-long steel fink trusses for $60 each, corrugated-steel factory roofing, Virginia greenstone siding, glass blocks, steel-mullioned windows, sewer grating, and even a manhole cover. These items would become the indigenous materials that would drive the design and form the substance of this small Kansas house.

SIZE 1,259 sq. ft.; COMPLETED 1991; LOCATION Franklin County, Kansas; DESIGNER/BUILDER Dan Rockhill, Lecompton, Kansas; PHOTOGRAPHER Hobart Jackson

THE **30-FT.-SQUARE HALF-** story sits at a 45° angle across the similarly sized first floor, creating unique, practical spaces both within and without the building. Outside, the overhanging corners of the second floor shelter the entryways. Shed roofs, supported by steel cables, cover the first-floor projections. Inside, the second-floor corner projections enclose a series of lofts.

Rockhill clad the first floor with steel roofing and the plywood box-beam kneewalls above with the greenstone, letting in light through a penetration of glass blocks. At the gable, he welded two trusses together, inserting glazing between the struts.

This small house...pushes the notion of "indigenous" to include the materials of...the salvage yard.

TO MAKE THE MOST OF THE
light coming through the
end gable, the living
room reaches roofward to
a cathedral ceiling. The
kitchen, furnished with a
salvaged high school home
economics class cabinet
set, tucks under the
cantilevered half-story.

A salvaged steel and
wood ladder leads to the
expansive master bed-
room/office loft, while
an uncharacteristic use of
sewer grating creates a
see-through railing. The
kid's loft at upper right is
reached via a length of
surplus scaffolding.

THIS CORNER OF THE FIRST
floor opposite the kitchen
encloses the kids' bed-
rooms. The slide-out,
translucent *shoji* screen
offers privacy without
cutting out light from the
core of the house.

BECAUSE THE SECOND FLOOR sits across the first at an angle, projections are created at each corner of the house. Here, the resulting loft offers a reprieve from the hectic life on the first floor of the house. The glass blocks suffuse the space with a soft, serene light.

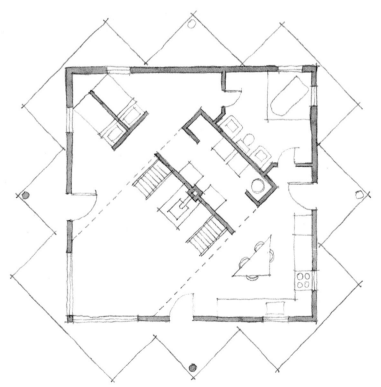

IF YOU'VE BEEN WONDERING where Rockhill used that salvaged manhole-cover grating, here's your answer. To give the kids—and anxious parents—a quick way to get from the parents' sleeping loft to the bedroom/play area below, the manhole grating provides a round opening through which one slides down on a long steel pole. With luck, the kids probably won't be able to shimmy themselves back up until they are old enough to lose interest. Otherwise, reinstalling the manhole cover itself is always an option.

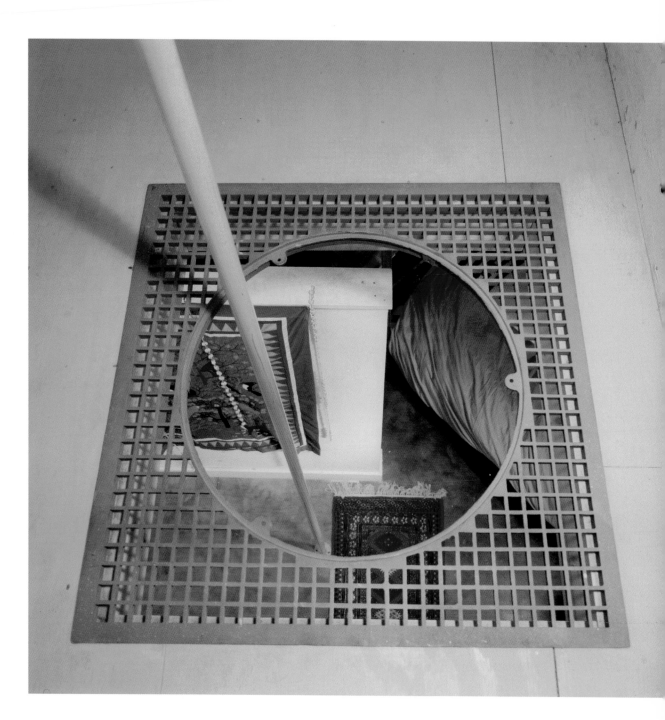

A Cottage off the Grid

FOR A STRETCH of more than 90 miles, Highway 1 veers away from the rugged northern California coastline, creating a dirt-road oasis of rustic living. Here on the "Lost Coast," it is not uncommon to find homes that are totally self-

sufficient for their power, heat, and water. This house by designer/builder Jim Groeling is this and more: It is a virtual showcase of fine, hand-crafted workmanship and indigenous materials.

The energy systems are decidedly nontraditional. Solar panels provide hot water and electrical power, while a Pelton wheel hydro-generator backs up the panels in the winter months. Advanced insulation techniques reduce energy consumption to a minimum. The result is a cottage that takes care of itself as it allows its owners to live a life unplugged from the grid.

SIZE 1,350 sq. ft.; COMPLETED 1985; LOCATION Petrolia, California; DESIGNER Jim Groeling, Petrolia, California; BUILDER Jim Groeling and Associates; PHOTOGRAPHER Carrie Grant

A RIOT OF COLORS in the front garden hints at the attention to lively details in the interior of the house.

Groeling oriented the house so that dawn light comes first to the kitchen, swings across the face of the house and its central living area, then settles at dusk to fill the bathroom (and a relaxing bath) with the glow of the sunset.

THE COVERED PORCH

with its generous roof overhangs provides shelter from the prodigious rains of the region. The brick and flagstone surface curves gently to provide relief from the strong rectilinear elements of the house, helping to meld the building to its site. Since the entry faces south, light bounces off the pale-toned porch to infuse the living room with soft light throughout the day.

a built-in seat offers a place to sit to remove shoes. The hanging cabinet, constructed of quartersawn white oak and fitted with "confetti" glass inserts, forms a gentle barrier between the dining area and the entry.

Both seat and cabinet are supported by a massive post entwined with vines hand-carved by Pieter Hudson. Meanwhile, living vines are working their way across the cabinet from a wall-hung pot.

THE 12-VOLT FRIDGE/FREEZER features wood doors and pulls to match those of the cabinets. Its pedestal contains a huge pull-out drawer. Mellow, but adequate, lighting is provided by 12-volt hanging incandescent fixtures and by abundant natural light.

THE KITCHEN CABINETWORK, designed by Groeling, was constructed from local white oak by Steven Applegate and Associates. Handmade pulls span the width of the doors and drawer faces, providing a generous grip, a pleasing appearance, and an implication of structural integrity for the joined-plank doors. The wood-burning cook stove sets at an angle across the corner, making good use of the space to run its chimney pipe.

and fine craftsmanship
are evident throughout
the house, as shown
by the curved balustrade
that leads elegantly up
the stairs.

Right: Handcrafted ele-
ments almost entirely
comprise the bathroom:
the built-in linen cabinet
of California walnut, the
shower stall made entirely
of redwood planking, and
an old-style claw-foot tub
set into a tiled enclosure.

CENTRAL TO THE DESIGN of the house, the massive fieldstone fireplace provides support for the heavy second-floor joists. Because the house is so well insulated and the fireplace is properly designed, it can easily heat the whole house. Heating coils set at the back fire wall provide supplementary hot water to the solar-heating system.

IN THE UPSTAIRS MASTER bedroom, a tiny, whimsical fireplace finds a nook in a brick and stone chimney that's gone a little wild before it regroups to exit the chimney. Protruding stones provide shelving for knickknacks and candles.

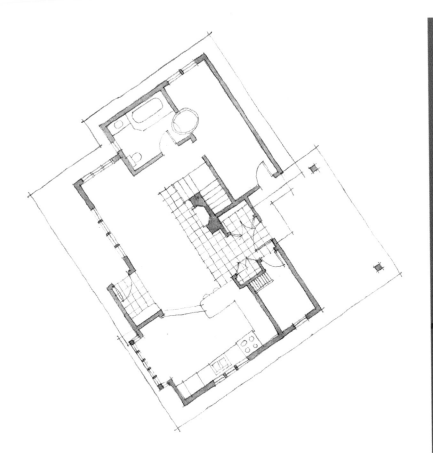

IN THE KIDS' BEDROOM
on the first floor, a built-in bed nestles into its own window nook looking out into the stone-bordered garden. The bed's generous side rail is crafted from a single waney-edge plank of California walnut. Drawers pull out from under the bed for linen and clothing storage, reducing the need for freestanding furniture.

The rounded wall protruding into the room from the left is the back of the circular redwood shower in the bathroom—though it steals some space, it does makes for a rather interesting corner.

Cottages

in Town

Along a tree-lined street, dappled light
flickering across the front yards
and gardens as children dart through
the gates of picket fences,
an in-town cottage offers a rich oasis
of serenity and security amidst
the hustle and hum of village life.

A Little Red House

THEY COULD HAVE HAD A CONDO, or they could have had a stock house plan off the builder's bookshelf, and they could have—maybe—saved a little money. But the owners of this little red town house in the Minnesota woods wanted a home that would not only suit their budget but also reflect their quiet, simple lifestyle.

Architect Robert Gerloff decided he could give his clients an energy-efficient, three-bedroom home with two full baths and a two-car garage—within their modest budget—if they would let simplicity rule the design. Given the go-ahead, Gerloff drew a plainly shaped cottage with all dimensions based on a cost-saving 4x8 grid, a trussed roof throughout, a siding-sheathed chimney, and standard-sized windows and doors specified for all openings.

Even with Gerloff's commitment to simplicity, he was still able to endow the house with a full-sized fireplace, French doors, generous porches, and numerous other touches that make the home a joyful and comfortable place to live in.

SIZE 1,780 sq. ft.; COMPLETED 1992; LOCATION Shakopee, Minnesota; DESIGNER Robert Gerloff (Architect), Minneapolis, Minnesota; BUILDER Laurent Builders, Shakopee; PHOTOGRAPHER John Danicic, Jr.

red for the exterior because it taps into the agrarian-Scandinavian roots of the region. And, like the structurally overscaled porch columns, the mono- lithic color scheme gives the house a sense of dignity and "presence."

The porch boldly projects out from the face of the building, serving both to de-emphasize the garage and to confer importance on the human-scale entrance that it encloses. The year-round side porch to the left balances the mass of the two-car garage to the right.

THE WHITE-PAINTED WALLS
and trimwork, as well as
the light maple flooring,
make the relatively small
"great" room feel full of
light and expanse well beyond its modest volume.

The French doors to the
right of the fireplace open
into a year-round sitting
porch made cozy with
wicker furnishings. The
window in the partition
wall opens to the study
off the master bedroom,
creating an overlook to the
living room and capturing
light and view from the
gabled windows on the
far wall.

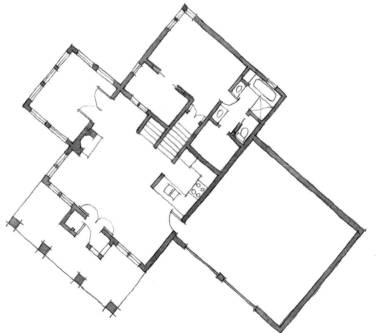

A STUDY CARVED OFF
from the master bedroom
closes off with paired
pocket doors, allowing
one partner to settle into
a cozy, late-night read
while the other sleeps
undisturbed.

ALTHOUGH THE KITCHEN
is inordinately small
(only 80 sq. ft.) relative to
the size of the house, the
U-shaped configuration
allows ample storage and
work surfaces. The square
tiles of the counter and
backsplash pick up on the
similar geometry of the
recessed-panel doors and
the square-shaped shelf
openings of the glazed
upper cabinets.

Only a wall at the end
of the sink counter sepa-
rates the kitchen visually
from the living room.

The Gray-Stone Cottage

THE CLIENT CAME TO house designers David Reel and Darlisa Black with a seemingly simple request: "Give me a modest-sized gray-stone cottage that will look like it has been here for centuries, heat it with a system that makes no demands on the earth's resources, and build it of nontoxic, recycled materials throughout." Reel and Black responded by creating a one-person stuccoed cottage on less than 800 sq. ft., using the money saved on volume to invest in a sophisticated solar-heated, floor-mounted hydronic system. This tiny home would be able to heat itself without the payment of a single monthly energy bill.

The walls are built with a relatively new construction material called "Ener-Grid"—a nontoxic matrix of recycled polystyrene foam encapsulated in a thin cement shell and shaped into building blocks. The blocks are covered with plaster on the inside surfaces and stucco on the outside. The builder shaped scraps of block and coated them with cement to create "stone" arches and quoins.

SIZE 768 sq. ft.; COMPLETED 1996; LOCATION Port Townsend, Washington; DESIGNERS David Reel and Darlisa Black; BUILDER Douglas Milholland, Blue Heron Construction; PHOTOGRAPHER Craig Wester

right on the ground on a
poured concrete slab,
comfortably nested into
its site. The builder broad-
cast crushed oyster shells
(an abundant local fish-
eries by-product) onto the
still-wet stucco to make
the surface finish appear
rougher and less reflective
—it looks as though it
has been through a hun-
dred years of weathering.

Quarry-stone-like blocks
surround the entry door,
arch over the windows,
and form quoins at the
building's corners, evoking
the traditional cottages of
the English Cotswolds.

from a nearby beach (one alder, one fir) flank an arched passage between the living room and utility room. The floor is not painted but gains its ocher color through a dye added to the concrete. There will never be a need to repaint to maintain the color.

A FOCAL POINT OF THE
diminutive kitchen, the recycled, self-draining cast-iron sink/drainboard sits in a countertop of marble pieces salvaged from a dealer's "boneyard."

The overhead cabinets run all the way to the ceiling, eliminating a dust-catching high shelf and adding storage space. To bring color and interest to the wall, the builder set a grouping of Mexican tiles into the plaster wall surface—a decorative touch that finds its way throughout the house.

THE PLAYFUL WALL MURAL
and trim detail were painted by the builder's wife, Nancy Milholland. As with the wolf head on the ends of the barge-board (see the photo on p. 176), it's the crafts-man's fanciful details that give this cottage its appeal. Mexican tiles are again used for decorative effect.

WHY LIVE IN A BIG EMPTY NEST when you can live a full life in a small, comfortable one? That was the question brought to Centerbrook

A Contemporary Cottage in Connecticut

Architects by a couple who had outlived their need for a family-sized residence. Although they had the money to build a house three times the size of the one shown here, they had more need for a house that was in scale with their new lifestyle.

Centerbrook responded by designing a house that was essentially one large room, with two corner areas that could convert to private spaces with the closing of a passage door. To ensure spaciousness, the main living area was graced with a cathedral ceiling and the center chimney was penetrated to reduce its mass and allow the passage of light.

SIZE 1,500 sq. ft.; COMPLETED 1985; LOCATION Essex, Connecticut; DESIGNER Centerbrook Architects, Essex, Connecticut; BUILDER Keith Nolan; PHOTOGRAPHER © Peter Mauss/Esto and *Metropolitan Home*

through the coarsely laid stone wall and into the geometrically rigid forms of the entryway, you are aware of the transition from the natural to the man-made. Downward-thrusting stickwork reduces the otherwise imposing grandeur of the towering gable. To each side of the entry, paired double-hung windows acknowledge the symmetry of the house and help balance its proportions.

Why live in a big empty nest when you can live a full life in a small, comfortable one?

you're greeted by the soaring, freestanding chimney. The opening in the chimney not only echoes the exterior form of the entryway and reflects the exposed interior framing but also allows you to see from one end of the house to the other. A pair of skylights clustered at the peak bring much appreciated light into the northern core of the house.

other side of the chimney, an abundance of uplighting infuses the living room with a warm, diffuse glow. The counter at left provides a subtle separation for the kitchen.

Beyond the chimney, the two corner rooms (a bedroom and a guest room/ study) are reached through wide passage doors. The built-in, glass-door display cabinets flanking each room entrance enliven the expansive walls.

THE BROAD WINDOWS on the south face of the house draw an enormous amount of light and warmth—not to mention our eyes—deep into the core of the house. You can't help but notice how the sash of the gable windows draws its forms from the roof framing exposed inside the house. This view of the house presents a delightful harmony of proportions, even down to the shape and sizing of the flat stones that create the terrace.

the terrace, the windows
of the great room seem to
embrace the ancient maple
at the edge of the yard.
In the summer, the shade
from this tree prevents the
house from overheating.

The molded trim detail
running along the perime-
ter of the gable helps tie
the window forms together
and fills an otherwise
drably vacant space. Warm
hues of furnishings and
the tile floor bring welcome
color into the space.

IN THE BEDROOM,
the sleeping area is flanked
by a pair of oversized
double-hung windows that
run to within a foot of
the floor, almost giving
you the sense that you're
sleeping outside. Felt
material covers the walls
to create an acoustic difference between this space
and the rest of the house,
making the room feel
quiet and restful.

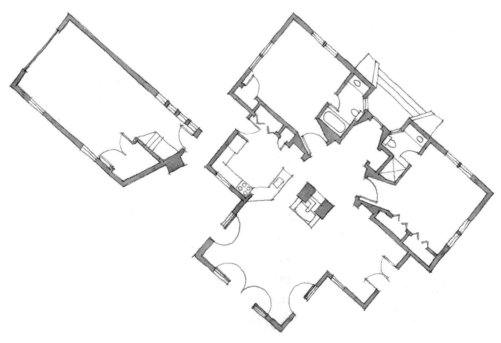

The Town Cottages of Stephen Wilmoth

STEPHEN WILMOTH

A S YOU DIP OFF U.S. 1 into the coastal villages of California's Monterey Peninsula, street after street of inexplicably small, unmistakably English-style town cottages greet your eyes. While the majority of these homes were built in the 1920s and '30s, a surprising number have arisen recently from the drawing board of architect Stephen Wilmoth.

A modernist by training and a traditionalist by temperament, Wilmoth is well equipped to meld his clients' seemingly contrary demands to create picturesque "character" houses that at the same time provide all the amenities of modern West Coast life, including ample natural lighting, useful exterior spaces, and a sense of spaciousness.

Wilmoth's homes succeed because he understands how cottage design elements function—not just how they are supposed to look. As a result, the charming and quirky elements ring true, rather than appearing tacked on, overwrought, or frivolous. A Wilmoth town cottage is more than an expression of its owners' storybook dreams: It is a rich manifestation of how they wish to live their lives.

(PHOTOS BY CRAIG WESTER, EXCEPT WHERE NOTED.)

WILMOTH'S COTTAGE DESIGNS are invariably compact, yet made lively with many jigs and jogs in the footprint and the use of various combinations of surfaces and textures in the wall and roof planes. Most draw on old-world cottage elements such as rubble-stone foundations and walls, small sash windows (often "trimmed" with flowerboxes or vines), a profusion of dormers, and decorative treatments that include a tasteful selection of moldings, shaped rafter tails and floor joists, and ceramic chimney pots.

WILMOTH MAKES MUCH USE of outdoor spaces, as in this hidden deck reached by zigzagging stairs on a tiled flat-roof section at the back of the single-story cottage shown above.

THE DRAMATIC ENTRY ARCH of the cottage below is mimicked by the door safeguarded in its shelter. The Dutch-style door is robustly made of thick tongue-and-groove, solid redwood planks. On the roof, the shingles are purposely laid unevenly to evoke the look of traditional thatchwork.

THE ENTRY OF THIS LARGER cottage penetrates deeply into the wall, creating a traditional, Gothic-style entryway. On the thick plank door, a "speakeasy" is protected by a hand-forged wrought-iron grate. Boston ivy, though only a few years old, is already closing in around the building as it reaches toward the Vermont slate roof to the right.

of window, outlined by a profusion of ivy, takes advantage of a tiny strip of wall between the corner of the house and a chimney.

WILMOTH'S CHARMING window treatments evoke the essential nature of the cottage. Here, leaded-glass windows are bordered by working shutters on wrought-iron hinges (above), by solid-wood framing and a miniature slate roof (left), and by effusive flower boxes.

ceiling of this cottage's dining room—a miniature version of a medieval home's great room—comes down to define the edge of the kitchen. Pine cabinets with raised-panel doors, an antique china cabinet, and a real butcher's block conspire to create a traditional-feeling, cottage-style kitchen. Stencils over the entry arch introduce the wallpaper in the dining area beyond.

PINE FRAMING AND PANEL- work, arching gracefully over the leaded-glass windows, imbue this reading room with a rich, warm glow. The surfaces of the bookmatched panels are handplaned to create subtle undulations that break up reflections on the broad surface—a finishing trick that gives the panels visual depth and a pleasing texture. The fireplace is of handcarved limestone.

BROAD FRENCH DOORS and sidelights make the courtyard a visual and instantly accessible extension of the living space. To each side of the doors, uplighting hides behind shell sconces—a theme carried through to the room's upholstery.

AN ELEGANT, FINELY CRAFTED stairway, the focal point of this cottage, sweeps from the living room up into a timber-framed turretlike space, providing access to the second-floor bedrooms and an outside roof balcony. Though broad, the stairway's 1½-in.-thick solid white oak treads offer absolute resistance to flexing and creaking.

wall surfaces give a rustic, almost beach-cottage feel to this master bedroom. To either side of the fieldstone fireplace, the board walls hide linen storage and audiovisual equipment (the battens double as pull handles). To the left, a bay window with window seat expands the space and brings in light and ventilation.

WILMOTH'S COTTAGES

are invariably a delightful blend of the old and the new—clearly exemplified in this stylish bathroom where an antique claw-foot bath tub is surrounded by a wainscoting of beaded-edge, tongue-and-groove boards. The wainscot jogs to accommodate the brass fixture hardware, showcasing the faucets and relieving the otherwise monotonous straight line of chair rail.

IN THIS BATHROOM,

a tiny arched window of leaded opaque glass, deeply recessed into the wall to create a shelf by the tub, brings in light and a good measure of charm.

The Cottage as Community

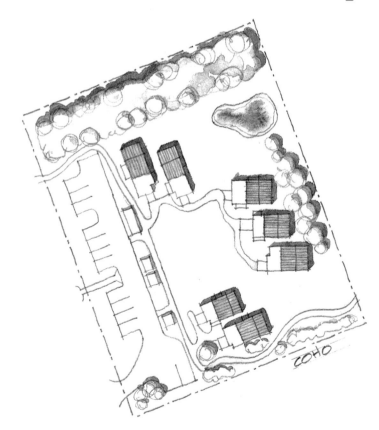

ABOUT A DECADE AGO, the late Rodney Morgan, a long-time Lopez Island resident and restaurant owner, had a bleak revelation: Seeing the cost of land and homes skyrocketing around him, he realized there soon would come a day when friends and employees living on a "family" income would no longer be able to afford to be his neighbors on the island.

Fortunately, Morgan's dark vision led to a bright dream: The idea of creating a trust to buy a lovely piece of land within walking distance of the island's commercial center. The trust would offer affordable building sites to people of modest means, enabling them to construct appealing, modest-sized cottages in an area otherwise shut out to them. Morgan's dream became manifest as the cottage communities of Morgantown and, a few years later, Coho. Here, in these clusters of cottages, the heirs of Morgan's dream live an affordable, engaging, and secure life in a community they care about.

SIZE OF UNITS 500 sq. ft. to 900 sq. ft.; COMPLETED 1992 to 1995; LOCATION Morgantown and Coho Communities on Lopez Island, Washington; DESIGNERS Robert Wardell of Lopez Island, Washington (Morgantown), Craig Webster of Seattle (Coho); PHOTOGRAPHER Craig Wester

would be appropriate to the traditional, rural setting of the island, the trust offered a variety of appealing, cottage-style home designs to choose from.

A central laundry and storage building would help keep individual homes small and efficient and spread out the cost of a generous utility room—a structure that would also serve as the community bulletin board.

The site plan called for the cottages to circle a common "village green" for sharing picnics, volleyball and, of course, yard maintenance.

...the heirs of Morgan's dream live an affordable, engaging, and secure life in a community they care about.

and careful handwork
make a delightful display
of shinglework on a gable-
end wall.

TO MAXIMIZE THE SHARED
open space of the com-
munity, the houses of
Coho are clustered closely
in groups. Careful orientation of most exterior sight
lines from within the
houses, however, affords a
sense of privacy. At the
same time broad, usable
porches draw people
outside and encourage
interactions with passing
neighbors. The absence of
car traffic makes the community eminently safe for
children and pets, not to
mention a parklike oasis
of calm for adults.

A WALK-THROUGH COMMON
storage building and a
hand-made fence buffer
the cottage community of
Coho from its centralized
parking area.

BY ERECTING A WALL at the "weather end" of her porch, this cottage owner expanded her tiny cottage into the backyard. It's almost a living room, a space she can enjoy throughout most of the year. An abundance of plantings march from the grounds onto the porch and into the living space. while her hand-built driftwood fence, free but for the effort, creates a private enclave.

AN ARRANGEMENT OF indigenous stones, effusive plantings, and a driftwood bench creates a magical landscape around the perimeter of this Morgantown cottage. A scene like this proves it doesn't take much money to create an environment in which one can feel a wealth of peace and beauty.

of the home shown below is apparent in the tiled hearth, the varnished maple plywood floor, and a finely crafted built-in daybed unit. All the cottages are constructed with a window alcove to provide an extra measure of light and space, but not all are taken advantage of in this way—it is up to the owners of the homes to do so.

OWNED BY A PROFESSIONAL chef who often freelances at home, this cottage enjoys a spacious, well-lighted kitchen with plenty of hardwood cabinets and a varnished mahogany plywood floor. This space is, in fact, the largest room in the cottage—and the one most often occupied. It goes without saying that the cottages can be as unabashedly individual as their owners.

IN THIS DRAMATIC INTERIOR, a "moongate" passage connects the living room and dining area. The oak trim that encompasses the opening was made by slicing the boards into thin strips and then glue-laminating them together against the circular framework. The ladder stair to the left leads to a sleeping loft and can fold back against the wall when not in use.

Rich in form, detail, and variety of materials, the entryway of this turn-of-the-century cottage near Santa Cruz, California, informs those who approach that this is indeed a special home. (PHOTO BY JIM TOLPIN.)

THE COTTAGE, even in its modest simplicity, can be a challenging house to design and build. Unlike the generic development rambler, a cottage is much more than a pile of man-made panel stock and preassembled components brought to a piece of ground and hammered together into a dwelling. Instead, those called to design and build a cottage must meet a larger purpose: to create not simply a house, but a place—a place that is in harmony with the earth upon which it sits, with the cultural heritage of the region, and with the people who will be blessed to inhabit it.

Inherent in creating this sense of place is remembering—or relearning—what gives a house the essence of "cottage": What it is about its form, the layout of its interior spaces, its architectural detailing, and its relationship to the surroundings that elevates it beyond just another small house.

In this final section, I offer some design suggestions for creating the cottage home. I begin with siting because a cottage must not only be a home unto itself but it must also be at home with its overall environment. Next, I move on to scaling

A 1930s cottage, designed by the Moody sisters of Monticito,
California, nestles idyllically amidst its gardens, hedges, and fences.

(PHOTO BY JIM TOLPIN.)

and shaping the structure, and then to interior layout strategies that can help make these generally diminutive houses feel more comfortable to live in. The latter is especially important, because in the small, compact house, the sizing of rooms, the alignment of sight and light lines, the utilization of built-in cabinetwork, the choice of trimwork and hardware, and the capture and manipulation of light—both natural and artificial—ultimately determine how livable the house will be. Finally, I discuss how a cottage can relate purposely to its immediate surroundings—how it can interact with its landscaping and gardens through extensions such as porches, verandas, trellises, and fences.

The cedar-shake roof, fieldstone chimney, and board-and-batten siding of this Carmel, California, cottage help integrate the home into its natural surroundings. (PHOTO BY JIM TOLPIN.)

Siting

In the past, simple cottage dwellings responded intimately with the environment. Since construction methods depended exclusively on handwork, it was much easier for the builders to go around tree roots and boulders than to work at removing them. The timbers themselves were often only partially squared or flattened, allowing some surfaces to remain true to the form of the tree from which they were cut. As a result, many timbered shelters featured curved, nonlinear elements that reflected the nonlinearity of nature itself—elements that we find so quaint and appealing in the archetypal cottages of the British Isles.

Of course, it is not always practical to work with curved timbers or to lay a house in the lap of the land, bending its surfaces to embrace each hump and hollow. And neither is it necessary, because there are other effective (and far less labor-intensive) ways you can help the cottage house evoke that sense of belonging and of being rooted to the landscape.

You can begin by making abundant use of indigenous materials in the siding, masonry work, and even roofing. For example, your choice of a cedar-shake roof and board-and-batten siding may be an appropriate gesture both to local resources and to the cultural heritage of the region. You can tie the house visually to a surrounding forest of tall trees by taking advantage of the strong visual signature of board-and-batten siding. You can choose a color scheme after careful observation of the site at different times of the day (and seasons, if possible) that melds the building intimately into the tones and hues of the surrounding landscape. And you can provide a sense of transition from a coarse, rock-strewn site to the flat, man-made planes of wall and window surfaces through the generous use of stone masonry in the foundation work and chimney.

To acknowledge a region's architectural heritage doesn't demand that your home follow in blind allegiance to any one particular historical style. Instead, it may take only the incorporation of certain historic forms and details to allow the house to recognize its roots and to feel in context

A progression of long-sloped, sharp-edged roofs, shingled siding, and rubble stone work in this new home designed by John Silverio of Lincolnville, Maine, pay homage to the ubiquitous turn-of-the-century Shingle-style "cottages" of the summer colonies along the Maine coast. (PHOTO BY BRIAN VANDEN BRINK.)

This cottage, designed by South Mountain Company of Chilmark, Massachusetts, engages its surroundings through its expansive deck, the stone step, and the extension of its rock foundation to enclose a flower bed. (PHOTO BY JOHN ABRAMS.)

with its cultural surroundings. In the cottage shown in the photo above, architect John Silverio drew from the forms and features of the traditional, turn-of-the-century Shingle-style summer homes that dot the shoreline surrounding the site. Though paying homage to this prevalent historical style, Silverio still took ample latitude in the overall layout and in many architectural details. Built more than 100 years after the island's first shingled summer cottages, this home responds both to a contemporary lifestyle and to the architect's personal visions.

A combination of compressed detailing (the tiny window and multiple panels) and a surrounding deep jamb and heavy stone case work help diminish the scale of this oversized Gothic-style door (designed and built by the author), making it feel quaint and less imposing.

(PHOTO BY JIM TOLPIN.)

While these strategies help root the cottage in the visual, textural, and cultural landscape, you also want to help the small cottage engage the landscape—to become spacious well beyond what its formal "footprint" might otherwise provide. This engagement comes through extending the house into the outdoors: Porches or covered terraces carry the floor out of the house and into the landscape itself. Not only will these extensions draw the house physically into the environment but they will also draw out the inhabitants as well, acknowledging one of the most essential and inherent joys of cottage life—the easy ability to interact with the natural world.

Thoughtfully using any combination of these design strategies, from the visual to the textural to the structural, should help you create a cottage-style house that gracefully embraces its surroundings.

Scale and Form

Part of the appeal of the cottage-style house is its human-sized scale. To quote architect Lester Walker of Woodstock, New York, "because of the tiny scale [of cottage homes], trees seem larger, nature seems larger, the car and other machines seem out of place, and people seem very important" (*The Tiny Book of Tiny Houses,* Overlook Press, 1993). The designers of Disneyland's Main Street were apparently well aware of this phenomenon: They scaled down replicas of classic 19th-century town houses to seven-eighths of their original size. The scale-down extended to architectural elements including door and window openings and trimwork. It's a subtle detail that few people notice, but it significantly alters their subconscious perception of the structures. As you walk down this fantasy Main Street, the buildings seem unexplainable more quaint and dreamlike, making you feel larger than life. And that, of course, is precisely what the designers intended you to feel.

This subliminal effect of scale reduction may explain the magical appeal of the archetypal cottage's diminutive details: their intimate entryways, tiny windows, and low ceilings. Used with discretion, a strategy of reducing the scale of certain portions of the building—such as minimizing the perceived size of a gabled wall by setting distinctive trim elements between a mix of siding materials (see the drawing on the facing page)—can add a good measure of appeal to the cottage-style house.

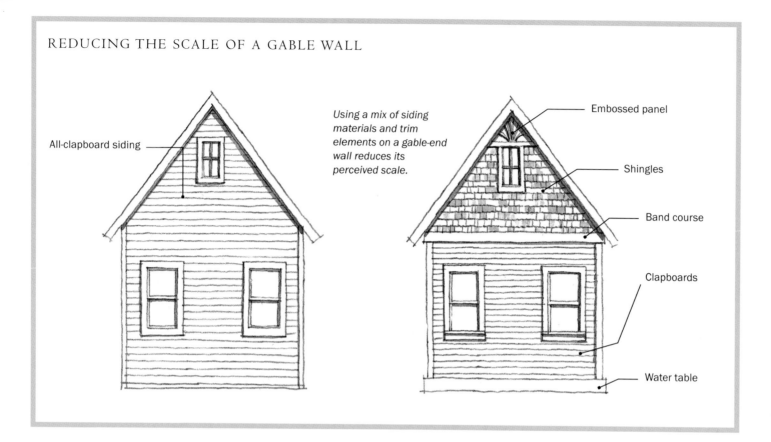

REDUCING THE SCALE OF A GABLE WALL

All-clapboard siding

Using a mix of siding materials and trim elements on a gable-end wall reduces its perceived scale.

Embossed panel

Shingles

Band course

Clapboards

Water table

SHAPE AND SYMMETRY

While certain shapes are more evocative of archetypal cottage architecture—the steep-pitched roof over a low, box-shaped form, for example—it is not necessarily the shape of the house that ultimately defines the cottage style. Indeed, there is often a degree of quirkiness in the shape of the cottage house.

Historically, the typical American cottage houses were invariably compact, rarely symmetrical, and almost never simply four-walled boxes supporting a roof. Instead, cottage-style houses abounded with bay windows, cantilevered reading and dining nooks, and the ubiquitous and useful porch. These details not only looked charming but they also added welcome spaciousness and utility to these modest houses without greatly expanding the foundation

Mid-19th-century cottages, such as this design by A. J. Bicknell, were commonly asymmetrical and full of jigs and jogs in the footprint.

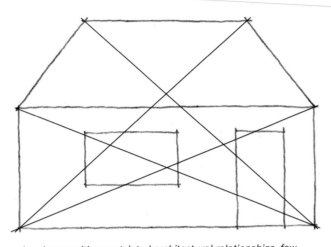

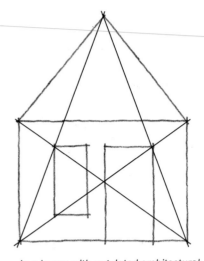

In a house with unregulated architectural relationships, few, if any, corners of windows and doors relate to intersection lines, disrupting the harmony of the overall form.

(ADAPTED FROM *HOME FROM NOWHERE*, BY JAMES KUNSTLER.)

In a house with regulated architectural relationships, the corners of windows and doors often relate to lines drawn through primary points of the house.

footprint (and thus the expense). Also, the proliferation of corners created opportunities for interesting exterior spatial relationships and, on the inside of the home, for clever, functional built-in furnishings. Corners also provided more room for windows—a boon for bringing more light inside.

But even with the cottage designer's love of quirkiness, it still seems necessary to balance proportions and to regulate the placement of the doors and window openings. Theories of symmetry and regularity in a pleasing building are not a new idea: From the first century B.C.'s Marcus Vitruvius to this century's Le Corbusier, renowned architects have expounded on the need to confer a fundamental geometry to the overall form and placement of a building's parts and openings—just as our bodies and components thereof are regulated. Unregulated architectural relationships can feel aesthetically disturbing.

In the drawing above, notice the fenestration of the typical contemporary ranch-style house: The invisible diagonal lines that create a subtle visual reference rarely intersect the corners of the window or door openings. In contrast, the diagonals on the gable end of a typical cottage-like house intersect the corners and edges of the fenestration in many places, helping our eye bring the elements of the house into pleasing agreement with one another.

ENTRIES

The entryway is generally the first architectural element people relate to when approaching a house. As such, it is one of the signature elements that define the house as a home. For visually, texturally, and psychologically, it is the entryway that welcomes people—and a cottage welcome must be warm and enticing.

The cottage entryway is mysterious, magical, and even profound; it evokes our curiosity, excites our spirit, and inexplicably draws us into the home. (PHOTO BY JIM TOLPIN.)

Consider the ranch house that presents its vast expanse of blank garage door, typically bathed in bright light, to any who approach the house. These doors predominate over the face of the building, overwhelming any other type or sense of entry. Also consider the oversized entry doors of grandiose neoclassic and contemporary-style houses. Their entries, greater than human-scale, are too often imposing, almost demeaning, and tend to make a person feel diminished and rather unwelcome. Now look at the typical warm and intimate entryway of the cottage where a softly lit, well-crafted door beckons you through a sheltering extension of the home. It is an entryway you want to go through.

The garage doors of this typical ranch house dominate the building, diminishing the human-scale entry. (PHOTO BY JIM TOLPIN.)

The picture window of this faceless suburban bungalow stares blankly at the street. (PHOTO BY JIM TOLPIN.)

The tall, narrow windows, exuberantly surrounded with rich trimwork, give this Victorian-era cottage a sense of personality and charm.

(PHOTO BY JIM TOLPIN.)

WINDOWS

Windows are an essential component in the creation of the cottage-style home. More than simply openings in the wall to allow light and view to come into the house, they can be arranged to enhance and make visual sense of the building's form. Furthermore, the need to relate the window opening to the wall surface creates an opportunity for distinctive ornamental elements. For substantial, detailed trim is not merely an add-on in cottage architecture—the boldness means something, it satisfies both the building and how we perceive it.

The shape of the windows may have considerable effect on cottage-style design as well. In his book *Home from Nowhere* (Simon & Schuster, 1996), architect James Kunstler proposes that horizontal windows are almost demeaning because they "frame the human figure in a way that implicitly emphasizes the non-public and intimate"—the human figure at rest. Few houses before 1900 had horizontal windows; they were introduced by "modernists" after the turn of century when changes in construction methods and materials allowed exterior walls to become skins, not necessary supporting members.

Basically, vertical windows make structural sense, in the same way as does the vertical structure of trees and our own bodies. In Kunstler's analysis, the windows of an appealing, human-centered home should be vertical or square, never horizontal because "vertical windows frame the human figure in an upright, neutral, and dignified way—reflecting back the human qualities that we project on a house to begin with." There's a practical benefit as well: Tall, vertical windows help capture the full richness of daylight (because it comes from more sources, from the sky to the ground)—not to mention allowing those inside to view a broader scene.

It does seem difficult for a home to conjure up a feeling of warmth and welcoming if it stares blankly at the street through a monolithic sheet of glass. In fact, one of the most endearing design elements of the traditional cottage-

The archetypal leaded, diamond-pane window helps capture the romantic essence of medieval English architecture. (PHOTO BY JIM TOLPIN.)

A vast view of the Strait of Juan de Fuca, Washington, is welcomed into the sitting porch/solarium of this 19th-century cottage through a wall of multi-paned windows. (PHOTO BY JIM TOLPIN.)

style home is its profusion of small-paned windows. Indeed, the diminutive, leaded diamond panes of Gothic-styled English cottages moved 19th-century architect Andrew Jackson Downing to proclaim them "so essentially rural and cottage-like, that the mere introduction of them gives an air of poetry to a house in the country."

But why should partitioned windows (and thus a partitioned view), seem so attractive and appealing? If we want a cottage home to bring us closer to its natural surroundings, why not go with a big "picture window" that essentially makes the wall evaporate? The answer is that partitioned windows help a cottage give its inhabitants a sense of protective enclosure while still helping them relate as intimately as possible with the cottage's surroundings.

A breakthrough book on thinking about houses in human terms—Christopher Alexander's *A Pattern Language* (Oxford University Press, 1977)—may help explain this phenomenon: Instead of putting us in touch with the outside world, large plate-glass picture windows actually tend to isolate us from it. Indeed, the big, uninterrupted opening of the picture window makes us feel exposed and vulnerable to the point where we may unconsciously shut out the view—or at least the sense of openness—it was supposed to afford us. Conversely, the small panes of sash-divided windows help frame the views for us, making them more intense, variable (each pane presents a slightly different viewpoint), and ultimately engaging. At the same

Second-floor windows should run low to the floor to provide a comforting view of the ground. Here, in addition to the dormer window, low windows are placed in the kneewall.

(PHOTO BY BRIAN VANDEN BRINK.)

Sunlight filtered through translucent cotton curtains infuses this cottage bedroom with a soft, serene glow.

(PHOTO BY BRIAN VANDEN BRINK.)

time, the presence of the sash itself (especially the thicker, traditional moldings) makes us feel sheltered and protected.

The placement of the window relative to the floor can be important as well. Most people feel more comfortable sitting by a window through which they can see the ground outside, not just the horizon or sky. On the ground floor, the windows should typically come to about 16 in. from the floor to accommodate this. On the second floor, where a high-placed window might only show the sky, low-placed windows are especially important.

People also generally enjoy the light and view through windows partially covered with curtains, surrounded by opaque tracery, or framed with vines on an outside trellis. Filtered light full of dancing shadows makes people feel cheerful; unfiltered light is much harsher and creates strong contrasts. We seem to feel cozier in soft, filtered light that shows more detail in the things around us—the kind of light that makes people appear warmer and softer.

A high-pitched roof, its ridge beam supported by timbered cruck-frames, provides more than ample headroom in the second-floor sleeping loft of this tiny New Hampshire cottage designed and built by Jack Sobon. (PHOTO BY BRIAN VANDEN BRINK.)

ROOF STYLES

With the roof sitting on the house like a cap, the structure appears bland and is less protected.

With a generous overhang, the roof embraces the house, sheltering its walls and windows and providing opportunity for structural ornamentation.

THE ROOF

Modern architecture is in love with flat roofs, but the simple pitched roof is still the most powerful symbol of shelter. (Ask any child to draw you a picture of a house, and you can be pretty sure you'll get a drawing of a single-gabled cottage.) Not only is the prominent, often high-pitched roof of the typical cottage house inherently attractive but it also provides a link to the past and to our gut-level instinct that says a firm presence of roof, both visually and physically, is essential to our feeling of being well sheltered.

Beyond providing a sense of well-being and security to the inhabitants, the prominent overhangs of an embracing roof also help you create bold shadow lines that define and make sense of the structural elements and overall proportions of the house. Overhangs provide an opportunity to install ornamental moldings and brackets—evocative details that draw our eye and pull at our heart. The drawing at right contrasts a cap-style roof and an embracing-style roof.

Designing the Cottage Roof

You can help a roof perform its magic—help it emphasize its promise to shelter and protect those who live within its embrace—by making it as large as possible. In the diminutive cottage, this is most easily accomplished by making it steeply pitched (which brings more of the roof into view from street level) and by allowing generous overhangs wherever possible. To break up the monolithic surface, give the roof visual interest by penetrating it with dormers—the more varied the better. Play with a combination of eyebrow-, shed-, or doghouse-style forms, but keep them relatively small and away from the roof edges (never extend them to the end) to avoid diminishing the dramatic impact of the roof itself.

Also consider these two basic design choices: You can cover the space uniformly under one large roof (such as the typical bungalow-style hip roof), a strategy that allows visitors to discover the interior spaces upon entering. Or you can define the interior spaces underneath a series of gables—the typical multiple-gabled neo-Gothic cottage. In the house in the photo at left, the series of gables shelters a corresponding sequence of second-floor bedrooms. A first-floor gable to the left encloses a cathedral-ceiling great room.

Rarely do cottage-style homes boast a full second story (and when they do, they generally cease to look or feel much like a cottage!). Instead, you can provide livable spaces under the roof by raising it a half-story on a kneewall— a much more economical solution than creating an entire second-floor wall system.

Typically, a series of steep gables provides ample-sized bedrooms, each uniquely shaped to the form of the roof above. And, of course, the higher the pitch, the more potential for additional attic storage over the second-floor bedrooms. A 15/12 pitch, for example, can provide a full-headroom storage area. It also opens up the potential for a dormer running along the roof to create a spacious living area.

The multiple gables of this wooded cottage, designed by Ginny Swain of Thorne, Gibson, and Swain Architects, Boston, Massachusetts, enliven the roof line while defining the rooms they shelter.

(PHOTO BY JAMIE SALOMON.)

A substantial roof overhang also protects the building—the more overhang, the more it shields the wall siding and foundation from the elements. If the roof cants toward the prevailing winter winds, it can direct the cold-air flow up and over the house, reducing heating bills.

There are more advantages: A large overhang helps keep the house cool in the summer by providing shade. In rainstorms, windows tucked under an overhang can be left open without letting rain into the interior. And overhangs visually and physically extend shelter into the spaces lying outside the walls. This helps integrate and expand the house—and, of course, those who live within it—into the immediate surroundings.

ORNAMENT

Cottage design gives a great deal of emphasis to ornamental details. Without these details, a house often feels too plain, cheerless, and devoid of life. On a practical level, ornamental trim elements help you define the boundaries of the major components of the house, giving them seams that help you bind the building together in a strongly visual, satisfying way (see the drawing on p. 218). Ornamentation helps us focus on details by allowing our eye to draw together and make sense of the larger proportional components of the house.

Look at the examples in the photographs at right: Why do the bold trim elements around the first arched window opening seem so appealing, while the near absence of trim on the second, similar-shaped window does not seem to feel "right"? One answer may be found in *A Pattern Language*, which proposes that our ancestors may have taken a cue from their own body structures (lips around mouths, protruding skull around eyes) when they thickened the openings around the doors and windows of their wattle-and-daub huts. As they no doubt quickly discovered, these

Surrounded by bold trim, the arched window above appears substantial and elegant. By contrast, the trimless, contemporary window at left seems merely pasted into the wall, appearing fragile and uncomfortable in its surroundings. (PHOTOS BY JIM TOLPIN.)

openings were indeed points of stress in the wall, easily breaking and threatening the integrity of the entire structure unless they reinforced them.

Later, to highlight the thickening effect of ornamentation, architects added profiles to the edges of moldings—the resulting shadow lines making them appear more substantial and satisfying to the eye. It doesn't take much. For example, simply adding a bead along the bottom edge of clapboard siding strongly reinforces the horizontal presence of the lower portion of the house, helping it feel broader, heavier, and more rooted to the earth. Conversely, adding a profile—whether a bead, a complex ogee, or even a simple rabbet—to both edges of vertical battens dramatically increases their presence, giving the surface to which they are attached a sense of height and lightness.

Abundant natural light, a cathedral ceiling, and a wide, open floor plan imbue this small Maine cottage designed by Rob Whitten of Portland, Maine, with a sense of warmth and spaciousness.

(PHOTO BY JAMIE SALOMON.)

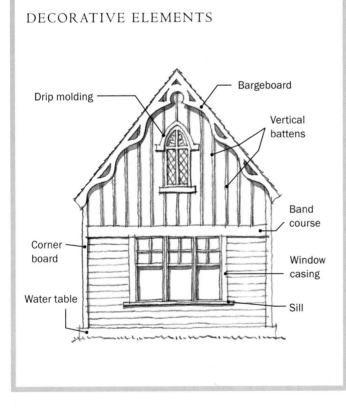

DECORATIVE ELEMENTS

Drip molding

Bargeboard

Vertical battens

Band course

Corner board

Window casing

Water table

Sill

Interior Spaces

The interiors of many contemporary cottages are surprisingly spacious. Judging from the outside of a house that abounds in diminutive architectural features and compact forms, you might think the inside will feel dark and cramped (which, in fact, many traditional cottages were). But few people today want to live in small, poorly lit rooms, cut off from one another. Instead, most of us desire as much light and space (or, at least, a sense of space) as possible. There is no reason that a cottage-style house, no matter how small or traditional in exterior appearance, cannot aspire to and meet these contemporary needs.

You can create the perception of spaciousness through well-lighted, open floor plans and the careful shaping of

COMPARATIVE FLOOR PLANS

(FLOOR PLANS ARE BASED ON THE "WORKINGMAN'S MODEL COTTAGE"
FROM DOWNING'S *ARCHITECTURE OF COUNTRY HOUSES*.)

CONTEMPORARY FLOOR PLAN

1840s FLOOR PLAN

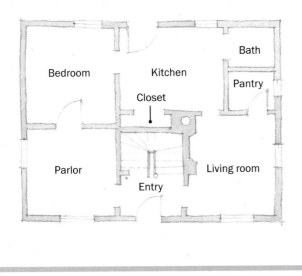

the rooms. Rooms can be joined for multipurpose uses, though areas can still be defined by changing the level of the floor or ceiling relative to the rest of the room. Built-in furnishings can give a house character and take wonderful advantage of limited space. And you can enhance the sense of abundant living space and further define areas through both the intuitive and thoughtful use of decor—not just the things, but their textures and colors.

FLOOR PLAN

The contemporary open floor plan creates spaciousness in the small cottage house in at least two basic ways: by allowing some rooms to expand to accommodate more than one use and by calling for lots of connections between individuated rooms. The open floor plan largely dispenses with

traditional passage doors, relying instead on half-walls, built-ins, and perhaps floor or ceiling level changes to define living and working areas.

Compare the two floor plans above of the same house. In the historical floor plan, the house (built during the golden age of plan-book cottages) is little more than a collection of individual boxes, gathered almost begrudgingly together under one roof. Each room is relegated to a single purpose, left to its own window(s) and doors for light and access. Unless a passage door is left open, the other rooms of the house might just as well cease to exist. Upon entering this house, you are immediately confronted with the limited welcome of a set of stairs leading elsewhere—you have almost no visual clues to what might lie beyond.

Now look at the revised, contemporary floor plan for this same house. The stairs are moved back away from the entrance, allowing you to experience more of the light and feel of the house upon entering. The kitchen and living room, separated by only a peninsula of kitchen cabinets, are melded into one spacious-feeling "great room"—though together they take up less space than they did as separate rooms in the historical plan. Even the parlor-turned-home-office can be joined to the great room by opening the French doors. The exterior French doors of the kitchen and bedroom open onto the same back deck.

In the new, open floor plan, the rooms more fully share the small enclosed space of this house, its light, its sounds, and its sights. The reduction of partition walls (though not enough to make the rooms totally lose their sense of func-

tion) and the subsequent increase of connectiveness amongst the rooms give the house a more rambling, informal, open feeling; this house will undoubtedly feel much larger and brighter than its 19th-century predecessor.

Fortunately for us, today it's easier to get away with building large, open rooms within a small house. As construction methods have changed, new framing techniques have freed houses from having to hang off a central chimney for support as did the traditional Cape and other 17th-century houses. Now we can easily support the structure without having to provide load-bearing walls and other supports throughout the interior of the building. Also, modern central-heating systems eliminate the need for providing each room with a chimney—or for closing off unheated rooms.

But having said that, it's well to remember that a cottage floor plan should still include one of the most essential ingredients of the cottage life: the hearth. Today we may not need the hearth for primary heating, but we do need it to create at least one place within our homes that feels emotionally comforting, hospitable, and, of course, bone-deep warm.

CHANGING FLOOR AND CEILING LEVELS

Obviously, creating a cathedral ceiling over at least one primary room can greatly increase the sense of spaciousness in the smallest of houses (see, for example, the photo on p. 218). It's quite a feeling to walk into a tiny cottage and suddenly be enveloped in a room full of height and light, allowing your spirit to soar to the rafters. It's unexpected and it can be delightful.

But tall ceilings can also sometimes be disconcerting. If the entire cottage is vaulted, there may be no place that truly feels protected, enclosed, and cozy. You may need to lower the ceiling (or raise the floor) to create a nook in certain areas of the house where people can feel cozy. In traditional cottage architecture, the inglenook (see the photo at left) provided this space in front of the fireplace.

Set just off the kitchen, this fireside inglenook provides a cozy sitting area where guests can hobnob with the cook. (PHOTO BY CRAIG WESTER.)

By dropping the floor in this living room, architect Stephen Blatt not only made the room feel more intimate but he also created a taller wall to accommodate an elegant bank of windows that draws the surrounding woods into the space. (PHOTO BY BRIAN VANDEN BRINK.)

There are other ways to make a small room feel spacious. One effective way is to raise the ceiling relative to an adjoining room (or rooms). This, obviously, gets you more head space—and more wall height to increase the vertical size of the windows. But changing the ceiling level also helps you define the room relative to the others without cutting it off with walls or partial separations.

You can also achieve that sense of differentiation (along with increased vertical height) without touching the ceiling at all. Instead, you can drop the floor, as shown in the photo above. From a framing standpoint, this maneuver may be easier and more cost-effective than fooling around with framing ceiling joists at different heights.

Varying floor and ceiling levels can do a few other things for you as well. For example, it can help you create a comfy nook within a larger room, making efficient and effective use of space. To avoid an unappealing, claustrophobic, closetlike area that no one would want to go to, you can make the alcove more inviting and cozy by lifting the floor up a bit to get it out of the traffic pattern (and up where it is a little warmer) and by lowering the ceiling (which makes the space feel more sheltered and intimate).

Architect Jefferson Riley of Centerbrook Architects in Essex, Connecticut, raised this nook off the great room, tucking it closer to the sloped ceiling, to create an alcove for intimate conversation and reading. (PHOTO BY BRIAN VANDEN BRINK.)

As you sit in the dining room of this cottage designed by architect Samuel Van Dam of Portland, Maine, unencumbered sight lines draw your eye within the house to the kitchen and living room and outside to the glorious marine view. Though the house is small, your visual sense of space is vast. (PHOTO BY BOB PERRON.)

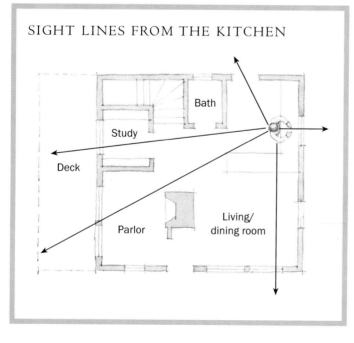

SIGHT LINES FROM THE KITCHEN

Bath

Study

Deck

Parlor

Living/
dining room

Playing with floor and ceiling heights can also help you define areas of transition within the house. For example, to create a sense of transition from the daily living areas of the house to the more private domains of the bedrooms, you can lower the hallway ceiling. Stepping down into a reading den lets you know that area is special, that it has a function different from the rest of the house. Likewise, stepping up to a dining area allows seated people to look directly at, not up at, people working in the kitchen. These strategies are effective in a house of any size, of course, but they are particularly useful in the compact cottage, where they can help define spaces and functions without creating barriers.

SIGHT LINES

Interior views can be just as important as exterior views for making a house pleasant to be in. When you are arranging the layout of the rooms, picture in your mind what you will be looking at when sitting, say, at the dining table or the living-room sofa. Your aim is to enhance the view from these places, so as to enrich the experience of being there. For example, in an intimate space such as a reading nook, most people like to look up and see what's going on in the world inside as well as outside the house. If interior views are limited or obstructed, people tend to feel out of touch with the life within the shelter.

You can make a compact cottage house feel more spacious by providing certain areas with abundant and lengthy sight lines. For example, orient the floor plan so that in certain places—such as the kitchen shown in the drawing at left—you can see most of the interior as well as outside in a variety of directions. If necessary, you can provide sight lines through hallways and doorways that open into other rooms.

Of course, it always helps to be able to see outside from many, if not most, of the places within the house. The effect on our sense of spaciousness is especially dramatic if the outside view is apparent immediately upon entering a room. But not any outside view may do—the more distant (and, of course, the more scenic), the better. To that end, think through the floor plan of the house relative to the site plan. Try to orient the layout of rooms, paying careful attention to where people will spend the most time, to take advantage of the best views and to draw them deep within the house.

BUILT-INS

Built-in furnishings contribute much charm, beauty, and practical function to the cottage-sized house. Often taking advantage of otherwise unusable or difficult spaces, built-ins appear—seemingly out of nowhere—as bookcases, bureaus, seating, side tables, and storage cabinets. In addition, you can use a built-in furnishing in place of a framed wall to delineate rooms. Not only do you get an effective partition, but you get a functional piece of furniture as well. In general, you'll find that building in the furniture means you can eliminate a surprising amount of freestanding pieces. Because the latter are more space hungry than built-ins, you can wind up with more open space in the floor plan—and thus a greater sense of spaciousness.

A built-in furnishing can do more than provide clever pieces of furniture or storage units, however. You can also use a built-in to create an enchanting space unto itself. An eating nook built into an east-facing bay window is an obvious example. And then there is the built-in window seat—no cottage should ever be without at least one. Window seats respect and serve people's need to enjoy the light and warmth that streams through south-facing windows. Without taking up nearly the room a lounge might take, the window seat offers a comfortable, attractive place to stretch out in the sun, a place close to the window so that you can see up to the sky and down to the ground.

Taking advantage of the otherwise awkward and limited space under the eave of a roof, this built-in bureau—designed and built by South Mountain Company of Chilmark, Massachusetts—introduces beauty and function into an upstairs closet. (PHOTO BY JOHN ABRAMS.)

A built-in window seat offers more than a pleasant place to sit in the sun: It maximizes the use of space by taking up less room than a sofa, it provides extra storage space for bedding (below the cushion), and the hues and patterns of its custom-made upholstery can enhance the decor of the room. (PHOTO BY BRIAN VANDEN BRINK.)

INTERIOR ARCHITECTURAL DETAILS

Writers of other books and magazines on cottages may disagree, but I think a cottage ultimately has very little to do with "cottage" (or "country") style decor. I'm not about to tell you what things to put into a small house to make it into a cottage house. Instead of decor as imported things, then, I'm going to consider decor as elements of the interior architecture of the house—and offer the following suggestions.

Go for the curves: It's nearly always beneficial to introduce curves into the shape and forms of the cottage interior. Our eyes like to follow curves, perhaps because it helps us link to the natural, nonlinear environment—and perhaps to those days when our shelters were not so rectilinear. For example, you can draw arches over prominent windows, or raise a vaulted arch ceiling in a dormer or a passageway between rooms. On a smaller scale, you can introduce curves into the built-in furnishings by arching rails and door frames. You don't have to go overboard (which is prudent because creating curves can get expensive)—a touch of curve here and there can provide a surprisingly dramatic effect.

Go for real wood boards to cover and form some surfaces. Solid wood softens the hard planes and edges of walls, ceilings, and floors and adds color, texture, and a good measure of visual interest. Narrow boards, especially with profiled edges, can help you define spaces: A change in textures implies that a certain area of the room is for a separate purpose. But you must also be careful not to

A carefully trimmed arched doorway—echoing the oval tub and sink—provides a pleasing transition between the vanity and bathing areas of a bathroom in a house designed and built by **South Mountain Company of Chilmark, Massachusetts.** (PHOTO BY JOHN ABRAMS.)

The handles of this vanity, handcarved from indigenous pepperwood, are indicative of the level and quality of detail in this finely crafted California cottage. (PHOTO BY CARRIE GRANT.)

overuse wood. Too much of it on walls, ceilings, and floors can be overwhelming and can make a house feel more like a rustic retreat than a modest, but elegant, cottage.

Go for quality where it counts. To me the cottage is about quality, both in the quality of the life it affords its inhabitants and in the materials of which it is built. Look around the interior of any house and ask yourself which objects you physically come into contact with on a daily basis. It is the doorknobs, the window and cabinet hardware, the faucets on the sinks. In the cottage house, these things shouldn't feel flimsy or look cheap. These things—at least on the scale of the cottage house—do not add up to a very large investment, but it is these details that can really make or break the quality of home you are trying to create.

At the same time, there is room for appropriate funkiness. For example, defects in flooring, as found in the lower grades of oak, maple, and pine, can work just fine when used judiciously. In fact, they help make the cottage feel unpretentious, informal, and interesting. You need only look at the endless monotony of clear oak floors of 1950s tract homes to sense the difference. And the money you save on the downgrades can be applied to crafting curves and obtaining quality fixtures.

LIGHTING

We like light inside a house—and usually plenty of it. Of course, you could easily satisfy that need by installing rows of fluorescent lights (just as they do in schools, shops, and offices). But lots of light from artificial sources is obviously not what you want in a place you're trying to make feel cozy and at home. Instead, most of us want as much natural light as possible during the day and a quality of light that softly mimics it at night.

Natural light During the day, ample daylight is readily available—all one need do is allow the light of day to enter the house. Design the house to gather natural light from as many directions as possible, especially from different portions of the sky and different reflected

Architect Rob Whitten of Portland, Maine, filled the gable wall of this cottage with multi-paned wood windows to infuse this relatively small house with an abundance of natural light. (PHOTO BY JAMIE SALOMON.)

Turn-of-the-century architect Bernard Maybeck brought uncommon elegance into the dining and kitchen areas of this house by installing narrow windows that run from the floor up into the roof structure.

(PHOTO BY RICHARD BARNES.)

surfaces from the earth. You have a distinct advantage in illuminating the small cottage house, since you can never be very far away from a wall—and thus a potential source of natural light.

Bring in direct rays of the sun by orienting some windows to the path of the sun, not just to a view. Ideally, try to provide each room with windows facing in at least two different directions. Not only does this enhance the quality of the illumination by mixing light from a variety of sources but it also makes a room feel much larger and less like a cubicle. The cottage house is responsive to this by providing far more jigs and jogs in its floor plan than most classic-style or ranch-type houses.

The typical tall vertical windows of the cottage also help draw in natural light. By reaching up high on a wall, light is brought deeper into the rooms and into the core of the house. Transom windows, though not especially effective for viewing scenery, are nearly always valuable for capturing more light.

To soften light coming through windows, you can, as mentioned earlier, construct outside trellises to encourage a veil of vines or add opaque tracery (stained glass) to the perimeter of the window. Other strategies include creating an angled window reveal to provide a reflective gradient from the brightness of the window to the darkness of the surrounding wall. It also helps to use natural fibers like cotton or muslin (which soften rather than reflect the light) as curtains. Finally, avoid placing glossy materials and objects in front of sun windows—the reflections can throw glaring, harsh light throughout the house.

Electric lighting In our earliest shelters, those of us foolish enough to stay up past sunset saw by the light of the cooking fire. This worked well enough to illuminate tasks close at hand, but the flickering, ground-level light made more productive tasks difficult at best. The discovery that the steadier light of torches, and later oil lamps, could be placed higher and nearer to the tasks at hand greatly expanded our productive hours.

In this house designed by architect Jefferson Riley of Centerbrook Architects, custom lighting fixtures are built into the furnishings. Light reflecting off the cherry wood surfaces fills the room with a rich, warm glow. (PHOTO BY BRIAN VANDEN BRINK.)

But the quality of the light did not change—our shelters continued to be bathed in a warm, soft glow that recalled the rich light of the sun. It wasn't until the advent of the electric incandescent bulb, and later the fluorescent, that primary illumination moved to the ceilings of our houses and work buildings. While these fixtures illuminated the space brightly and uniformly, the quality of light became harsher and colder, throwing shadows that created sudden boundaries of light and dark. A house lit with overhead lighting, even full-spectrum light, cannot provide the diffused, warm glow dear to cottage life.

I find that the best way to light the cottage house electrically is to use indirect lighting for general illumination and directed task lighting for reading, food preparation, and craft areas. Indirect light, which can be mounted on walls or hidden behind ceiling trim, infuses the space with a soft, diffuse light that eliminates harsh boundary shadows. A dimmer switch aids in selecting the right amount to balance against available natural light. The direct light, which can be provided by inoffensive, ceiling-mounted spot lamps, gives you full intensity light only where you need it. Craftsman-made fixtures can add charm and individuality. To ensure a rich infusion of diffuse, warm light, use shades made of natural materials. Also be aware that the colors of the predominant surfaces in the room—wood floors, painted walls, and rugs—also affect the hue of the ambient light. Lean toward reds, browns, and yellows, which add warmth, and stay away from blues and grays.

Landscaping and Exterior Spaces

What is a house without some form of garden, without flowers or vines growing near or upon it, without porches or terraces that flow enthusiastically into its surroundings? It's still a house, but it isn't a cottage.

THE GARDEN

The cottage garden, almost by definition, is enchanting and beautiful. Sometimes wild, often unkempt, rarely formal, never pretentious, the cottage garden lets us know that the people who live there participate—let's even say rejoice—in that home's natural surroundings. Needless to say, they also enjoy having fresh vegetables, herbs, and flowers just a step or two away from the kitchen door.

I'm not a gardener, so I won't attempt to tell you how to create the essential cottage garden (if there is such a thing), but I would suggest that you think carefully about where to place the garden. Beyond accommodating good soil and access to sunlight, also consider how you will feel in the garden space. If it's behind the house, will you feel too iso-

A luxuriant garden is one of the defining features of a cottage home.

(PHOTO BY BRIAN VANDEN BRINK.)

EFFECT OF LANDSCAPING
ON THE PERCEIVED SIZE OF A HOUSE

Abundant vegetation close by the house
reduces its perceived size.

lated from the community of life flowing by the front yard? But would you feel too exposed moving to the front? Perhaps a side yard would give you the best of both worlds. In any case, try to locate the garden—at least your herb and vegetable one—close by the kitchen door.

LANDSCAPING AND FOLIAGE

Ideally, a cottage house nestles into the natural, or seemingly natural, flora of its site. I'll let Andrew Jackson Downing explain why: "Cottage architecture, especially, borrows the most winning and captivating expression from foliage…no architectural decorations, however beautiful or costly, can give the same charm of truthful decoration to a cottage as flowering vines and creepers…[for it is the]…vines on a rural cottage [that] always express domesticity and the presence of heart."

There are the practical sides too. Foliage proliferating over a house helps reduce the scale of the building, drawing it toward the ground and allowing it to blend harmoniously with its site (see the drawing at left). Also, sunlight filtered through foliage is soft and comforting when it enters the house. Foliage can also help frame a view, drawing our attention to it and increasing its pleasure.

OUTSIDE "ROOMS"

By extending into its environment, a house becomes far larger than its enclosed space. Well-defined extensions such as porches, decks, and earthen terraces draw people out of the house, giving them an enjoyable place to merge with the outside. They allow the cottage, and cottage life, literally to expand in the warm seasons. These outside spaces also draw the house itself into the adjacent surroundings, helping it participate more fully with the site while anchoring the building to the earth. This increase of useful floor space comes at a cost, of course, but far less of one than if you were enclosing the space on a full foundation wall behind insulated exterior walls and roof. Outside rooms are one of the most economical ways to make a house feel—and be—larger than its footprint would otherwise promise.

The most popular extension (and perhaps one of the most indicative cottage elements) is the porch. Unlike the modern deck, the sheltering porch can truly become another room of the house, especially if fitted with screens in summer and storm windows in winter. But to work well, the porch must be deep enough to hold furniture and people in a way that allows them to converse if they wish to. That means it must be at least 6 ft. deep and 8 ft. wide to provide room away from the traffic pattern to the entry door. You can increase the porch's sense and function of shelter by enclosing an end—perhaps partially with a trellis. This breaks the wind, captures sun heat, and increases its privacy. For still more privacy, consider the second-floor porch. Because of the viewing angle, your visibility to the street or neighbors is lessened or outright eliminated. It can function as a private outdoor space—and as an added bedroom in certain seasons of the year.

THAT INFAMOUS WHITE PICKET FENCE

In the popular mind, the archetypal cottage always resides behind a white picket fence. Ever think about why it's white; or why it's a picket, or even why there is a fence at all? The answer to the first question is easy (assuming I'm right, of course): White paint was less expensive than many other colors, and it lasted longer than darker colors that absorb more light and heat from the sun. There are only so many Tom Sawyers in one town.

The answer to the second and third questions addresses the nature of cottage life itself. While a fence helps the cottage define the yard, the subtle, almost decorative pickets soften the sense of enclosure, making the fence feel less abrupt and imposing. As the house sits in quiet repose behind the picket fence, its entryway framed behind an arbored rose-covered trellis, the fence helps the house capture the space immediately around it, calling it its own. It serves to remind those of us outside that a rich and reflective cottage life goes on behind this gentle white barrier—a semi-private life not necessarily or implicitly cut off from the community around it.

A turn-of-the-century cottage on Martha's Vineyard, Massachusetts, boasts two porches: an extensive first-floor porch that expands the home's living room into the life of the community and a smaller, more private outdoor sitting and sleeping space tucked under the second-floor gable. (PHOTO BY BRIAN VANDEN BRINK.)

A Carmel, California, cottage sits behind a classic picket fence that defines the street boundary without making the home feel entirely cut off from the community. (PHOTO BY JIM TOLPIN.)

architects and designers

Cottages by the Water

FISHERMAN'S CAMP COTTAGE
(pp. 30-33)
Joe and Mary Lou Upton
Vinalhaven, ME 04863

NANTUCKET "BEACH BOX"
(pp. 34-39)
Botticelli and Pohl Architects
Zero Washington Street
Nantucket, MA 02554
(508) 228-5455

FAR WEST BEACH COTTAGE
(pp. 40-45)
Andy Neumann
888 Linden Avenue
Carpenteria, CA 93013
(805) 684-8885

DOWN-EAST, DOWNSIZED, SHINGLE-STYLE COTTAGE
(pp. 46-51)
Samuel Van Dam
(Van Dam & Renner Architects)
66 West Street
Portland, ME 04102
(207) 775-0443

FROM PUMPHOUSE TO BEACH COTTAGE (pp. 52-59)
Geoffrey Prentiss
(Prentiss Architects)
1218 6th Avenue West
Seattle, WA 98119
(206) 283-9930

COTTAGE ON THE POINT
(pp. 60-65)
Stephen Blatt Architects
10 Danforth Street
Portland, ME 04112
(207) 761-5911

PLAYHOUSE BY THE SEA
(pp. 66-75)
John D. Morris II
Architects/Land Planners
89 Elm Street
Camden, ME 04843
(207) 236-8321

COW ISLAND CAMP COTTAGE
(pp. 76-81)
Rob Whitten and Will Winkelman
(Whitten Architects)
37 Silver Street
Portland, ME 04112
(207) 774-0111

COTTAGE CLUSTER EAST
(pp. 82-93)
Richard Bernhard and
John Priestley, Architects
22 Central Street
Rockport, ME 04856
(207) 236-7745

Cottages of the Forest and Mountains

AT HOME ON THE FOREST TRAIL (pp. 96-101)
Ross Chapin
Box 230
Langley, WA 98260
(360) 221-2373

TINY TEMPLE IN THE WOODS
(pp. 102-105)
Arlene Tunney (Tunney Associates)
306 Pine Orchard Road
Killingworth, CT 06419
(860) 663-2019

TWIN-GABLED FOREST COTTAGE (pp. 106-111)
Jim Sterling, Architect
94 Commercial Street
PO Box 7305
Portland, ME 04112
(207) 772-0037

FRENCH HUNTING LODGE IN THE PACIFIC NORTHWEST
(pp. 112-115)
Jack Jackson
Eastsound
Orcas Island, WA 98280
(360) 376-4057

COTTAGE MADE OF LOGS
(pp. 116-121)
Timothy and Elizabeth Bullock
RR #3
Creemore
Ontario, Canada L0M 1G0
(705) 466-2505

ISLAND COTTAGE ON SPEC
(pp. 122-125)
John M. Campbell, Architect
PO Box 237
Orcas Island, WA 98280
(360) 376-2035

COTTAGE CLUSTER IN THE WOODS (pp. 126-131)
Peter Kilpatrick
1800-A Lake Road
Friday Harbor, WA 98250
(360) 378-5404

Cottages in the Field

LITTLE HOUSE FOR A BIG MOUNTAIN (pp. 134-139)
Geoffrey Prentiss
(Prentiss Architects)
1218 6th Avenue West
Seattle, WA 98119
(206) 283-9930

MODEST COTTAGE ON THE VINEYARD (pp. 140-143)
South Mountain Company
PO Box 359
Chilmark, MA 02535
(508) 645-2618

**ISLAND COTTAGE IN STONE
(pp. 144-149)**
Olson Sundberg Architects
(Project Director: Joshua Brevoort)
108 First Avenue South
Seattle, WA 98104
(206) 624-5670

**STONE COTTAGE REVIVAL
(pp. 150-155)**
Centerbrook Architects
(Principal Architect: Chad Floyd)
Box 955
Essex, CT 06426
(860) 767-0175

**SALVAGE-YARD VERNACULAR
(pp. 156-161)**
Dan Rockhill
Rt. 1
Lecompton, KS 66050
(913) 864-4024

**COTTAGE OFF THE GRID
(pp. 162-169)**
Jim Groeling
(Jim Groeling and Associates)
Box 168
Petrolia, CA 95558
(707) 629-3320

Cottages in Town

**LITTLE RED HOUSE
(pp. 172-175)**
Robert Gerloff (Architect)
4007 Sheridan Avenue South
Minneapolis, MN 55410
(612) 927-5913

**GRAY-STONE COTTAGE
(pp. 176-179)**
Doug Milholland (Builder)
343 35th Street
Port Townsend, WA 98368
(360) 385-6525

**CONTEMPORARY COTTAGE IN
CONNECTICUT (pp. 180-185)**
Centerbrook Architects
(Principal Architect:
William Grover)
Box 955
Essex, CT 06426
(860) 767-0175

**TOWN COTTAGES OF STEPHEN
WILMOTH (pp. 186-195)**
Stephen Wilmoth, Architect
4114 El Bosque Drive
Pebble Beach, CA 93953
(408) 625-5399

**COTTAGE AS COMMUNITY
(pp. 196-201)**
Robert Wardell of Lopez Island,
Washington (Morgantown)
Craig Webster of Seattle (Coho)
Contact: Community Land Trust
PO Box 25
Lopez Island, WA 98261
(360) 468-3733

Note: The Institute for Community Economics in Springfield, Massachusetts (413-746-8660) publishes a handbook on creating Land Trust communities in the United States, of which there are currently more than 200 and many more in proposal.

BOOK PUBLISHER
Jim Childs

ACQUISITIONS EDITOR
Julie Trelstad

ASSISTANT EDITOR
Karen Liljedahl

EDITOR
Peter Chapman

DESIGNER
Carol Singer

ILLUSTRATOR
Mike Kowalski

TYPEFACE
Centaur

PAPER
Warren Patina Matte, 70 lb.

PRINTER
R. R. Donnelley, Willard, Ohio